THE FICTION EDITOR,
THE NOVEL,
AND THE NOVELIST

THE FICTION EDITOR, THE NOVEL, AND THE NOVELIST

Thomas McCormack

ST. MARTIN'S PRESS

NEW YORK

Design by Robert Bull Design

Library of Congress Cataloging-in-Publication Data

McCormack, Thomas.
    [Fiction editor]
    The fiction editor, the novel, and the novelist / Thomas
McCormack.
        p.   cm.
    Previously published under title: The fiction editor. c1988; and
published in London in 1989 under the same title as above.
    Includes bibliographical references and index.
    ISBN 0-312-11467-2
    1. Fiction—Technique.   2. Editing.   I. Title.
[PN162.M35   1994]
808.06′83—dc20
                                                                94-25772
                                                                CIP

First Paperback Edition: October 1994
10 9 8 7 6 5 4 3 2

to
Sandra

The Best Sensibility

CONTENTS

Thank you Roy Gainsburg, Ridley Pearson, Jessica Kovar, Bill Thomas, Bob Weil, Mike Sagalyn, Mark Levine, Charlie Spicer, Lincoln Child, and, of course, Sandra McCormack, for reading and commenting on the manuscript.

Thanks, too, to Wendy Kaplan for typing the manuscript.

To my colleagues George Witte and Peter Ginna, who listened, read and edited with courtesy, patience, intelligence, pertinacity and sensibility, I owe a special expression of gratitude.

THE FICTION EDITOR,
THE NOVEL,
AND THE NOVELIST

"Editors are extremely fallible people, all of them.
Don't put too much trust in them."
—MAXWELL PERKINS, *to an author*

"Who's Coaching the Coaches?"
—*Runners World* editorial

"These souls are very few; and of these few, not more
than ten are of the best."
—RUDYARD KIPLING, *Kim*

The hook intro: The greatest secret factor in American fiction in the past half-century has been the fiction editor, and, by a huge margin, his history has been one of opportunity either lost or actively destroyed.

The straight intro: This book is about the fiction editor's job—what he can and cannot be expected to do, and what abilities and training he needs to do it.

The upbeat intro: The fiction editor who has the needed talent and skills can be a combination doctor, teacher, coach, and conscience who could benefit any writer who ever lived.

Editors do four things. They *acquire* (go out and find authors, manuscripts, and book ideas, and sign them up). They help *publish* (influence the promotion, the jacket, the selling tactics). They *support,* comfort, and retain authors.

But the job they're classically identified with—and which has always felt to me their quintessential role—is their work on the manuscript. They *edit.* I'll focus solely on that assignment, and solely on novels.

The editing of a novel has three stages: reading, analyzing, and prompting revision if it's needed. Each stage calls upon special abilities in the editor; the later stages depend on the earlier; and the one (complex) gift needed throughout is what we can call 'sensibility'.

1

READING
AND
SENSIBILITY

First comes reading. The good editor reads, and he responds aptly, where 'aptly' means 'as the ideal appropriate reader would'. This responding depends on *sensibility*—the apparatus within that reacts to what's immediately given—a good (or bad) sentence, a vivid, exciting (or blurred, flat) scene; it's the sensor that feels fear, hope, curiosity; that registers dismay, joy, relief; that purrs in the presence of wit and drama and poetry. The good editor's sensibility is such that he's gripped, bored, delighted, confused, incredulous, or satisfied in the same place as the appropriate reader would be. This quality, sensibility, is absolutely essential. Without it, the editor with a script is like an ape with an oboe: You can be sure no good will come of it, and the most you can hope for is to get it back intact. It's the one element in all editors that you—where 'you' can be writer or publisher—must *demand*.

Be slow to say there's no such thing as an 'ideal appropriate reader', because there's a useful sense in which most of us accept there is. Consider: If someone gives you the latest Pynchon novel and seriously says "Just the thing for the Agatha Christie fan," you decide he's crazy, but not because you reject the concept of 'the Agatha Christie fan'. Christie and Pynchon may share some fans, but it's a sure thing their two readerships aren't totally identical. It's the publisher's awareness of the damage an inapt sensibility can do that tells him, when he's received the manuscript of an orthodox manor-house mystery, not to assign it to an editor who can't enjoy Christie. That editor doesn't have the right sensibility. He won't respond aptly.

That sounds so reasonable, it almost seems vacuous. But it leads to a basic postulate: *The only valid measure of an editor's sensibility is the degree to which his responses replicate those of the appropriate readership.*

This doesn't entail vile pandering to static and formulaic taste. The 'appropriate readership' needn't be any familiar class from the past—the 'Christie fans', the 'Michener fans'. When Ezra Pound was editing T. S. Eliot's *The Waste Land,* he was bringing to bear a literary sensibility that was acute, fresh, and without label—but it wasn't unique. If it had been truly unique, it would have been useless, damaging, to Eliot. In fact, there were many readers whose responses were similar to Pound's. Pound and Eliot, editor and writer, were lucky in each other.

There's no way other than by reference to reader response to justify editorial comment. Even the elitist Pound would agree with that. (It's true that editors often phrase their justification in terms that suggest absolute standards—they call for 'balance' or 'leanness' or 'resolution'. But these qualities aren't intrinsic virtues; where they're desirable—and there are times when they're not—it's because their absence is producing unwanted effects on the book's appropriate audience.) The sermon from James Joyce's *Portrait,* or the Legend of the Grand Inquisitor from Dostoevski, would, like diamonds in the roast beef, obviously be inappropriate for *Tom Sawyer*—

but the 'obviously' is justified only by the predictable impact on the appreciative reader.

Even when confronted with something altogether new, the right editor can respond to it aptly—where to be 'right' means to react as its *possible* audience would, however unmapped and undefined that congregation has hitherto been. The right editor—as Pound was for Eliot—is right not because he has some sort of absolutely good taste, a special insight into literary Platonic forms. Nabokov, a reader of exuberant and joyful responsiveness, despised Faulkner, Mann, and Camus. Did Nabokov lack 'good taste'? You can't think so if you've heard his appreciations of Austen, Dickens, and Tolstoi. It doesn't take 'good taste' to respond to Faulkner. It simply takes a sensibility that responds to Faulkner. And, since there is a large audience of non-editors who respond approvingly to Faulkner at his best, an apt editor for him did something valuable for author, readers, and publisher. (Faulkner fans may want to convey *why* he is enjoyable—to them—but this line of pursuit always leads ultimately to their saying about a certain facet, "I like this," to which an infidel, someone of a sensibility that's different but not necessarily base, can simply respond, "Well, I don't." The infidel should not edit Faulkner.)

To help grasp the implications of sensibility in an editor, ask: How does it go wrong, and what's the result? The first way a 'wrong' sensibility in an editor shows itself is in either misplaced disapproval or misplaced admiration. The inaptly critical editor—without ever getting to analysis and revision, which he would surely mishandle—will reject books that he shouldn't.

Imagine a job applicant coming in to you, the publisher, and spending the first fifteen minutes trying to impress you with his sensibility by declaring that Follett's *Needle* is boring, Roth's *Letting Go* dull, Wouk's *Caine* trash, Lee's *Mockingbird* simpleminded, Tyler and Updike too precious, and Mailer and Clavell too coarse. If you're looking for a general fiction editor, you should end the interview quickly with this literary Torquemada.

This isn't to say that every editor must be evenly responsive across the whole spectrum of fiction. I enjoy James Gould Cozzens's *By Love Possessed* immensely, but I realize that its rococo style is neither good nor bad in the eyes of an Artful God in Heaven. It isn't wrong for a private person to recoil from that style. The publisher, however, though he shouldn't require that every editor love it, should see it as a terrible failing if an editor's spectrum is so narrow and rigid it blinds him to the possibility that Cozzens has an audience. The publisher—and you, the writer or reader—can require that the editor have sufficient vision to prompt him to pass the Cozzens on to another editor and say, "It's not for me, but I suspect there may be something here." Every couple of years it's revealed that some justly celebrated book was rejected in manuscript by a dozen publishers. Most publishers have the good sense to be pained if they learn that their house was one of the decliners.

At the other end of the axis is the editor who'll accept anything above a certain low threshold of literacy, and so issues scores of titles aimed at a readership—people who would buy these books and enjoy them—that's close to nil. The author may feel a fleeting pleasure at initial acceptance, and a paper manufacturer somewhere smiles, but thereafter follows nothing but disappointment.

The damage an editor with bad sensibility may do is even more poignant if a good or potentially good book is *signed up* by him. He can miss or disdain the worthy stuff in the book, and prize the worst. The inaptly critical editor will eventually kill with mad surgery: Let's relocate the heart, replace the brain, cut these legs off just here. His polar opposite will beam hearty approval and sing 'Happy Birthday' as the script turns blue and expires for want of the merest first aid.

Misplaced criticism trajects beyond the book to its author. Recently I read a manuscript of a first novel that at its best had a style as rich, graceful, subtle, and marrow-deep as Nabokov's. When I told the author this, she was almost shaking with relief: Her first would-be editor had told her to cut out all the palaver and get on with the story. And in a crisis of confidence she was beginning to think he might be right.

An editor like that is destructively incompetent. In my time in publishing I'm convinced I've seen several talented young writers misled down the road to oblivion because they fell into the directing hands of editors who, despite high reputation, articulateness, and a desk-side manner painted by Norman Rockwell, had disastrous reading sensibilities.

The editor who is indiscriminately approving does harm in a different way. He won't kill the author, but he won't supply needed help during the writer's labor, and many books will be stillborn because he hasn't spotted remediable faults. Every editor corrects *something*. But catching eighty percent of the flaws isn't enough if the most important ones are among the remaining twenty and the book is dying because of them. Editors have a right to feel unfairly treated if they're blamed for a bad book when in fact they had reacted against the final twenty and asked the author to change them and the author wouldn't. But no amount of other hard work acquits them if the truth is they never recognized the fatal twenty as flaws at all.

If, for the novel's ideal appropriate reader, the story falters because of a key incredible sequence in the narrative and the editor says, "I didn't *mind* that"; if the book fails because its readers find the hero repellent, and the editor says, "I thought he was interesting"; if a book feels flat and vaguely stupefying because not one of the major characters comes to a fate that follows from anything the character himself did, and the editor says, "But that's like life!"; and if every ideal reader, every bookseller, and even you and I attack the ending as ludicrous, and the editor says, "I *loved* the ending; I think it *had* to be that way"—then our conclusion has to be that he should not be a fiction editor. As a private person he'd be entitled to any responses whatever. But as an editor it's essential that he have responses that reflect those of the appropriate audience.

This apt reaction should occur on every level of the book. The editor-as-reader should feel pleasure or satisfaction where broad macro-elements like plot and resolution are got right, but he should also delight in the writer's good performance all the way down to the choice of individual words. In certain novels, the diction is as great as in poetry (the typhoon scene from *The Naked and the Dead* was anthologized by Seldon Rodman in his *One*

Hundred Modern Poems), and if the editor can't react on that micro-level, he'll never be good enough.

Given this rough (and interim) notion of 'sensibility', now add:

1. The sole fact that someone is an editor is no proof that he has apt sensibility. People come into publishing for reasons that are easy to confuse with having the right equipment. High literacy is not sensibility; high grades in comparative literature certainly do not entail sensibility; and a high desire to write is sometimes flatly antagonistic to the kind of reader-responsiveness needed.

2. After they're in publishing, people too often rise to editorship on inadequate evidence. In their own houses, they get such jobs because the editors they worked for have moved on; or if they win editors' desks in other houses, it's because of the books their résumés say they "worked on"—with no examination of the work they *did*. Some employers have the good sense to ask candidates to read test manuscripts, but there are tight limits on how much these quick tests can assay—and besides, who's to say the judging employer has any sense?

3. An experienced editor can almost never be brought to see that his sensibility is defective. There are several reasons for this. He can always point to *some* editorial judgment he's made that Pound and Perkins would agree with, and this sustains him: See? I *do* have sensibility. Second, no matter if a response is so deranged it belongs on a microscope slide, he can always find *someone* who supports it: See? John agrees with me.

Third, and perhaps most surprising, he doesn't necessarily ever get fired. Authors may love him: With warmth, patter, and quiet confidence, he convinces his writers they're in good hands; they praise him to their agents, who, wanting to keep their most successful authors content, send them to the editor. With valuable writers thus thrust upon him, the editor is a good acquirer, his books make money—and that's all his boss has to know. Nobody ever examines his editing. They presume it must be terrific because good editing is what makes an editor famous, no? In this way the editor spends a deleterious career—a stone-fingers who thinks himself a catcher in the rye—and no one ever knows it.

4. Because the later stages of editing—analysis and repair—depend on the earlier, *everything* depends on sensibility. Without it, whatever further work the editor does on the script will be either feckless or poisonous. If an editor can't register symptoms, he certainly can't identify the healthy or treat the ill.

5. In an adult, the lack of apt sensibility is incurable. It cannot be taught.

PART TWO

DIAGNOSIS
AND
CRAFT

On to analysis—which might better be called *diagnosis*. One difference between a private reader, whose responses can be right-on, and an editor should be this: The editor ought to be able to *identify what is causing the response.* The private reader may be unengaged, deflated, frustrated, or baffled by a book—but he probably can't specify what events, passages, lines, very words, are making him so. Anyway, why should he have to? It's not his job. It *is* the editor's job.

If the first stage of the editor's 'examination' (his reading and responding) uncovers 'symptoms' (undesirable effects in the apt reader), then and only then he should go on to the second stage—diagnosis. Diagnosis entails the use of technical tools and tests to track back from the symptoms to the faults that are causing them. It's an essential part of the editorial procedure, it's the first thing the editor must do after reading and responding, and it's a far more difficult task than most editors, publishers, and writers suppose.

The very term *diagnosis* prompts the first comment: The editor should embrace the old doctor's maxim: First do no harm. Be wary of even applying technical diagnostic tools to a well manuscript; such diagnosis tends to lead to treatment—which can only harm a healthy specimen.

But assuming the script is *not* perfect, the assignment

now is to specify *why* not. First, express the symptoms—the undesirable feelings, impressions, convictions the reader has. Second, pinpoint what in the script (or missing from the script) is causing them. Then stroll on to treatment—see Part Three.

Which makes it sound far simpler than it is. And in fact it's constantly assumed to be a simple thing by most of the industry. Senior editors who know too little about the demands of the job blithely turn a manuscript over to assistants with virtually zero instruction. The policy implies: Anyone who can read can edit; just go through the script and tell the author what you think. As in other medicine, most editorial malpractice stems not from conscious disregard but from obtuseness: a blunt ignorance of what's involved.

One tip-off that difficulty lurks here is this observation: Next to how *slow* they are, the single most frequent gripe by authors about editors is, "When he talks to me about what's needed in my manuscript, he's rambling and vague." The reason for this is seldom that the editor is too polite to be indelicate; instead it's that—despite possibly having an adequate sensibility—he has no *craft*.

To see what fiction-editing craft might be, start by looking at the faults it's intended to detect. There are two kinds, whose difference can be suggested by calling them the *dermal* and the *internal.* The dermal is local, here-and-now. You can cite and label it like a public blemish. You can point at specific words that constitute it.

It is immediate—the moment you encounter the cause in the script, and the moment you sense something's wrong, are all but identical. Most dermal faults do not produce delayed reactions.

These blemishes lie right on the surface of the novel, and they include failures of diction, grace, freshness, materiality, credibility, pace, vividness, understandability, interest. The dermal components—blemishes and triumphs together—because they *are* on the surface, don't require special craft to detect. They require diligence, solid training in English, a good sensibility. Given these qualities, any editor can tweeze, scrub, and buff, so that at least the skin of the script will be acceptable to the eye.

Diligence is required because the potential *number* of dermal blemishes is immense. A reader's responses are all but uncountable. He reacts, however fleetingly, to each word, to its combination with other words, to their sequence—and so on up through sentences and paragraphs to the largest structural elements of scene, character, plot, and coalescence. It's a forest of turf, bush, and trees in various sizes, shapes, and species—made more teeming by a swarm of smells, sounds, and flickering wildlife.

To notice, remember, and organize them all is a daunting task. Of course you don't have to go through all these steps on the dermals and record them in a ledger. Clichés; repetitions; stale modifiers; abstract generalities where concrete specificities are needed; phrases, images, and metaphors that simply misfire— these can be red-penciled on the page *en passant* during the second read.

(The *second.* Rarely should a book be edited on only one reading. A pencil may be close by on first read, but used only to flag quick items. Reading fiction with a pencil *in hand* the first time through vitiates apt response.

For example, some editors, during their first reading, do such things as write a list of the characters, their descriptions, and a diagram of their relationships. This helps the editor to keep things clear. But the private reader doesn't do this, so the editor has disjoined his own reaction from that of the audience.

Such editors will often then base their editorial remarks solely on their many notes. This yields a second example: Suppose something early in the novel turns out to be irrelevant. It would not have been flagged the first time through because the irrelevance wasn't evident at that time. So it will never be flagged. There are lots more reasons why a one-reading edit is inadequate, and serious writers should be disturbed if they know it's happening to them.)

Surface faults may rattle like sleet across the narrative, which means they require unrelenting alertness, but their very noisiness and immediacy can preoccupy the editor and distract him from deeper things. Editors are commonly caught up by the gaudiest flaws in a script—say, one scene that fails entirely, a singularly defective character, and a bad ending—and they're driven with alarm to mend these hemorrhages; once that task is done, they sag back in relief and satisfaction—the novel is saved!—while lesser or more hidden lesions bleed the book pale.

The largest, the most basic faults, the *internal* failures, don't betray themselves with one smoking phrase. They don't, in general, lie on the surface of the novel. They can't be recognized at once as faults. They may have no obvious fixed address in the manuscript; often, indeed, the problem is that something has been omitted entirely. And often they are composites, an element becoming a flaw only because a succeeding element doesn't consummate: A failure of promise entails both a promise and a lack of fulfillment.

Some symptoms of these diffuse, internal ailments in a novel are a disappointed sense of its not meeting us at the station, of its having missed some unnameable opportunity, of its lacking a life-supporting temperature, of inertness, of inconsequence, of meaninglessness to events, of something, somewhere in the book, gone profoundly awry.

Their causes include faults in the original setup of situation and cast; the misuse of 'accident'; incoherence of 'theme'; defects in the characters' purpose, effort, action, promise, achievement, and interconnection. Since these causes don't lie on the surface, they're harder to identify, like a missing vitamin, an allergy, a secret spinal bend. The patient lives, but is listless and halt. And, woefully, the patient's doctor often doesn't see the condition as something wrong and remediable: We wish he had more snap, but that's just the way he is. The diagnosis of these ailments requires more than dermatology. Identifying the bug, the chemical imbalance, the anatomical fault, can defy the most determined scrutiny if the examiner relies solely on intuition. What's needed is an analysis that is canny, informed, fundamental, sensible, technical, systematic, and thorough. What's needed is craft.

A stipulative definition of *craft:* It is that part of former art that is now so well understood it has been anatomized and codified, and therefore it can be taught and systematically applied. Perspective in drawing, close-ups in film, flashbacks and juggled points of view in writing were all once new, arcane and thus artful. Today they're basic elements of craft, routinely part of any studious practitioner's equipment. All craft was once art.

If that's craft, then fiction editing currently has almost no craft at all.

Almost nothing about it has been codified. There is no textbook. So it's not taught or systematically applied.

Any pursuit—creative or otherwise—in which the craft is rudimentary will, despite flashes of intuitive brilliance, produce results that are for the most part formless, chaotic, incomplete, and unsatisfactory. Which is currently the prevalent condition of fiction editing throughout the world.

Generally, inadequate editors don't want to hear this. That's understandable. If someone says to us, "You know, regardless of how long you've been at it, you really have no systematic grasp of the fundamentals of your job; you're winging it all the time"—we bridle. The old Senior Editor's first response is usually, in effect, to deny that the job has any fundamentals.

He'll say, "I don't think there should be rules for creative work." You dance and jabber that your point is not to tell the author how to write right; but if it's written wrong, it's the editor's job to tell him where and how it's wrong. With his remark, Senior Editor is confusing the craft of editing with the craft of writing. If it ain't broke, don't fix it, but if it *is* broke, someone's got to perceive that fact and say what needs fixing. This is diagnosis, and diagnosis does have fundamentals, and those fundamentals, codified, would compose a major part of the craft of editing.

(Listen closely, and Senior Editor will on occasion be heard complaining that certain writers he handles have never bothered to learn their craft—and he'll say this without ever seeing the implication. It's as though an obstetrician were to criticize the gestating mother for not knowing the 'basics'—right diet, exercise, no smoking—while maintaining that *his* work should be carried out solely on instincts, with no training or method. Keep listening and you'll also hear his outrage when the author's husband or neighbor horns in with editorial suggestions. "Lord save us from amateurs!" he'll wail. Meaning people who lack the craft he says doesn't exist.)

Or he'll say, "No two books are alike." Well, no two human beings are alike, but they can both have measles. Two errors *can* be alike, and, in truth, even the most anarchic of editors knows this and recognizes generic flaws. If an editor reads ten murder mysteries and they all feel unsatisfactory in the same peculiar way, and the peculiar way seems to be connected with the fact that they all neglect to tell whodunit, he is overmatched if he doesn't at last generalize from this. He may primitively declare that murder mysteries had better tell whodunit or risk reader dissatisfaction; or he may frame a higher generalization about *promises* in a script, and how, if the writer makes them, he'd better fulfill them. A while ago there was a script about a large family that lives in an old wooden house, in which the first three times we see one of the children, he is playing with matches—in his room, on the back stairs, in the cellar. Nothing ever comes of it. Except that the reader, however unconsciously, registers discontent. No two plays are alike, but in orthodox narrative, Chekhov's rule still applies: If the author brandishes a gun in the first act, he had better fire the thing by the third. (Fulfilling all promises shouldn't be confused with answering all possible questions—as it is in a popular instructional by John Gardner.)

Made naked like this, it seems undeniable that there are such things as generic dangers that could be specified in a manual of craft. "Oh, that sort of thing is obvious," says Senior Editor, "you shouldn't need a manual to tell you that." Which is a foot stamped in the right direction because it stops talking about no two books being alike.

But, like a witch doctor growling at Dr. Schweitzer, he'll still resist conceding that there is, even theoretically, a textbook that he would be a better editor for having read. "Your instinct is your textbook," he'll flick fractiously, without grasping that instinct is sensibility, which means that it's essential but it's not enough. *The critical difference between instinct and craft is this: Instinct tells you* that *something is wrong, but it won't necessarily tell you* what *is wrong.* To believe that instinct needs no supporting craft is like believing that so long as a would-be doctor has eyes and ears, he needn't be burdened with medical school.

The last line of resistance Senior Editor will take when queried about the alleged absence of craft in his work is simply to deny that it's absent, assert that he knows all that stuff, that any experienced editor does, and that to codify it would be as ridiculous as codifying how to get up and get dressed. Which is what allows him to figure that even an untrained assistant can do it.

I maintain *nobody* can do it adequately without training, without craft; and currently there's nowhere to get that craft. Recall my earlier lines about how editors land their jobs, in which I suggested their elevation had little to do with the degree and quality of the most important element they bring to the job—their sensibility. This is even more true of their skills at diagnosis. There are too few publishers with the time, the awareness of the need, and—most to the point—the *ability* to examine in detail the specific work editors do on manuscripts. It's impossible to evaluate an editor unless you are familiar with the original script and with what the editor said to the author about it. Too often the boss will simply look at, say, a ten-page letter from the editor to the author and conclude, "Ed really worked on this one!" But the question is: Was the work any good? Long, hard work is essential to achievement in editing, and, as a group, editors spend as much time on their job as any professionals I know, but though overtime is necessary, it's not sufficient. A sedulous editor can frisk every line of a book, and relieve it of a thousand harmful oddments; dazzled by such accomplishment, he will never accept that he may still be less than competent at his job. (Keep in mind that, throughout this jeremiad, the indictment of the editor is solely that he isn't as good as he ought to be—which is certainly true of most of us, no matter what we're doing. And that most of us are like Senior Editor in that we are grimly guarded, not to say hostile, when anyone questions our competence.)

The problem begins with the fact that young editors are taught very little, and nothing systematic. When they are assistants, the explicit tutelage from their bosses is usually confined to the other major aspects of the occupation—acquisition, 'publishing', handling authors.

When it does have to do with analyzing the script, it's

likely to be fished out of a meager and idiosyncratic black
bag of editing tricks the editor has collected. Each editor
tends to have certain diagnostic specialties of his own—
particular sorts of faults that he is highly alert to, and is
wont to name again and again. Usually he has picked up
these singular long-suits randomly—because of a personal bent of sensibility, or an early egregious flaw he
once stumbled on in a novel, or some other accident of
education (which is to say that editors are disposed to
have a *style* almost as authors do).

But 'random', in an apprenticeship, is tantamount to
fragmentary, sporadic, shallow, and short. It's all right
that no two editors are the same—no two doctors or
coaches or singing teachers are exactly the same. But it's
a sign of something wrong when the contents of these
editorial black bags are so sparse, trinkety, and various,
with few common instruments to be found in any two of
them. They call to mind a convention of 'sensitives',
clairvoyants all of whom take as their basic lead the personality before them, but each using for the ceremony of
his reading his own preferred conjuring device—cards,
leaves, stars, Ouija.

If the would-be editor is not going to hear it from his
boss, where *is* he going to hear it? And the very few
experienced editors who will admit they don't know
enough about technique but would like to—where do *they*
go? There is no guru, no handbook, no Julia Child cas-
sette.

First I must concede—more than concede, *celebrate*—
the fact that the Few have been among us, and that there
have been instances of Lazarus the Scrivener made to
take up his book and walk because of the insight of a

gifted editor. Over the years, the industry has been grati-
fied by distant rumor of specific prodigious editorial
achievements, and it's informative to note how often they
have been occasioned by gargantuan manuscripts, tales
that have overflooded the banks of all reasonable narrative: It meant the editor had to reduce three thousand
pages to fifteen hundred, and thus it required that every
segment come forth and declare itself, show its papers,
justify its presence. Paradoxically, the editor was forced
to a more particular and systematic scrutiny than a more
pocket-sized package of chaos would ever provoke.

And there have been other truly book-saving performances by editors. But—except in the cases where the
hobbling flaw is so obvious that any diligent reader
would spot it—it's a rare thing, usually the result of a
happy match between failing and forte: The ailing book
has found its singular specialist. Old Senior Editor, who
hates first-person novels for wrongheaded reasons he
can expound sagely, is at last presented a sick manuscript
for which indeed the correct remedy is a conversion to
third person. A legion of writers will give testimonials
about their editors, but my argument is not that editors
never diagnose anything; it's that eighty percent isn't
enough. Though, in accumulation, the array of correc
tions may seem wondrous to an author, he is as unlikely
as the editor ever to be aware of the twenty percent
missed.

And the undetected faults probably include most of
the important ones. Why? Because the reason many of
them are undetected is that they are deep internals, and
this means they're likely to be fundamental. Half a dozen
times a year we read a novelist's fervent acknowledgment

of his editor's contribution—only to encounter in the
novel itself remediable infirmities of such undeniability
it's hard to figure the writer was told about them and just
refused to fix them.

With this as background, I now need to be more
specific about the sorts of things I claim editors should
know but don't. The form of what comes hereafter in
Part Two will be the citing of subjects within this craft,
a sprinkling of ad hoc specific editing principles, and at
least one display of what a 'systematic' editing device
would be like.

Part Three will suggest still more ways in which craft
would be helpful, and in the Notes thereafter I'll describe
in greater detail one or two of the basic tools. These
scraps won't begin to amount to the textbook; they're
meant only to convey the vast range of craft that has
never been codified, or even thought through, and to
indicate its complexity, its learnability, its limitations.
Above all, I hope to persuade you of its utility, its immense potential importance.

A slog through thirty or forty books about the craft
of writing fiction reveals several things. First, you come
away feeling that none of them qualifies as an adequate
summary of the subject. Often you can read an entire
book and discover just one piercingly useful remark. Second, each of them is stunted by aesthetic prejudice (usually unsuspected by the instructor himself), by confusion,
and by blindness to certain essential questions. Third,
they all share a tendency to blur the distinction between
the *novel* and the *writing of* the novel. You can sympathize
with this to an extent, because of course the aim of the

how-to part is to help the student create a certain thing, and if he doesn't understand the thing, the skill-instruction can be vacuous and directionless. I'll eventually need to clarify the implications of this murky charge, but the immediate point is that almost all of the subjects touched on (and they are seldom more than touched on) in how-to-write books should be subsumed in any textbook on editing. In other words, a portion of it should consciously be devoted to the *thing,* the biology of the novel, before passing on to diagnosis and treatment.

Among other things, the textbook should lay out diagnostic methods—general systematic procedures for doing medical workups on various parts of the novel's body. And it should also catalog all the symptom-specific tips that can be garnered from the best editors.

And then—as we'll see under Revision—it would teach the editor how to coach the writer who wants it, not just about what *result* he should be after, but about how to get it, how, so to figure, to position himself, hold the racquet, place his feet, approach the ball.

All this and more, but let's start by taking a typical aspect of biology, the simple name of which will bring a tolerant smile to the face of skeptics who by now are lying in wait.

Take point of view. Editors will breezily comment that POV is child's play, that naturally one is on top of simple stuff like this. But one is not. POV is far more subtle, complicated, and permeant than the average editor ever suspects. He will say, "Well, naturally you don't change the point of view abruptly, or three times on a page, so the reader doesn't know where he stands." He will say this, but then seldom notice explicitly when it is done: Every week you can buy a published novel sharded by just such blunders. But POV is more than a question of holding the camera steady. And it's even more than the basic question of where to position the camera in the first place—though you regularly see novels miscarry because of an error in choosing first or third person, or the wrong 'eyes', or the wrong distance. Regardless of what POV is chosen, there is an almost unlimited density of sensation available to the lens—but it does not all pass through. The author imposes a filter, some part of which is natural to him and essentially unalterable; but another part is alterable at will, and when it is changed, the effect on the reader can be profound without his ever being able to specify the cause. I know of two novels of recent times that were seizingly successful right up to the final act, where an almost subliminal but nevertheless suffocating tightening of POV cut off a vital supply to the brain—and stunted the books. The authors have told me that in neither instance did the editor comment on this in the script. If you switch from Jane's POV to John's to Ralph's to the dog's and the result is like a dropped deck of cards, the editor may notice. But if, while maintaining Jane's POV, you zoom back so far it has changed from 'third person character-view' to 'third person remote-limited'—the reduction in the 'personal' things he is hearing may give the editor a vague sense his partner seems different these days, and he may even register a new formalness to her demeanor—still he is unlikely to think it's his duty to judge whether this is a good or bad sensation to give the reader, and he's even less likely ever to trace the cause back to specific POV filterings. If the rich flow of detail through 'her eyes' perseveres, but no longer contains in-skull reports of feelings and intentions, the sensitive reader will feel it, albeit without being able to name explicitly what's happening. In the two recent novels I mentioned, the reader feels the way he would if, without a word of harshness or explanation, he were quietly 'dropped' by a friend.

These effects can be conveyed only by demonstration. The good textbook would take a number of scenes and retell them from half a dozen points of view. And in case the distinctions are missed, it would spell out the differences in impact on the reader. (Similarly, the most telling way to teach appreciation of *style* is not simply to present great samples; follow them with rewrites that are not parodies, but are simply flattened, with the greatness taken out.)

Not one editor in a thousand approaches the grasp of point of view conveyed in *The Rhetoric of Fiction* by Wayne Booth—a college teacher. (And even that commendable book neglects whole species of effect. I am sometimes melodramatically seized by the somber vision of potentially the best editor in the world teaching college composition in Geneva, New York, or Hornell or some town or another in that section of the country.)

None of this is meant to say there's never been an editor with a single generalized insight that he could bring to bear in his work. Here's an example of a principle from a celebrated editor of a generation ago, William Sloane:

"The enemy of fictional density is the one-thing-at-a-time scene, that simply shows you, the reader, one of the facets of the story, whether it be something about the characters or about the action or the setting, or whatever.

All too often this thin scene is invented to convey a piece of factual information to the reader—a tea party where the characters talk about their ancestors and their families, and, perhaps, as an added fictional bit of icing on the cake, announce that a new teacher is coming to town. [But in] a good piece of fiction . . . all parts of each scene are working: characterization of the people, creation of the physical world of the story, narrative motion, whetting of anticipation, resolution of the mystery, characterization of the author—style inevitably does this—all the dimensions, and all at once."

This amounts to a symptom-specific diagnostic tip a good editor will have at the ready; when a scene feels papery, it can be one of the first medical workup tests that the editor applies, just as coaches in golf or tennis, on observing a typic bad result, will immediately look for the typic flaw in technique that usually causes it.

Here's a second principle, a first cousin to Sloane's, tailored to address a particular feeling the responsive editor may register in the last chapter of a novel. The symptom is a feeling of attenuation, enfeeblement. The cause may be *serial resolution.* It can arise in novels with, say, more than three central characters. Each is wrapped up all right, but one by one. Bridey betrayed Kevin to the British because he preferred her rival, Kate. She confesses at the end to Sean, who has married Kate. The intent of the scene is to reveal that she hates herself. Sean then confesses to his brother his relief: He's feared Kate had done it. Kate, miserable and angry because her hometown thinks she's a traitor, finally gets a letter from her aunt: The truth is out and the aunt begs forgiveness for her bad thoughts.

Parsed that way, its revision seems obvious: Let's have one colossal scene with all parties present. Expressed as a general rule of writing, this says: Resolve simultaneously if you can; it makes the narrative exponentially more powerful, and it tends to take on a life of its own, distinguished from the author-driven serial wrap-up. (This principle is one that technicians in film and theater have always seen better than those in the business of fiction.) But now we should underline that it is not a 'rule' for writing; there have been serial resolutions that have worked, and the editor must have a sensibility that will not be prevented by his intellectual grasp of the craft from realizing when a serial resolution is working and should be left alone. Which means that it's not a 'rule' of editing either; it says only that, if the ending feels feeble, consider the possibility that the cause is serial resolution—but also consider other causes, just as a doctor, aware of certain general symptoms, will test for a variety of possible ailments.

Another symptom-specific diagnostic tip: If the editor senses lethargy in the first fifty pages of a novel, he should look for a *premature flashback*. Unless it's a great story in itself, don't expect the readers to be interested in a character's background before they're interested in his foreground.

Now let's work our way toward more general, systemic tools for editors. This requires comprehending a cluster of elements that precipitates much of the narrative in orthodox fiction. It's a cluster that editors know too little about. And yet a better understanding of each of its elements, and how they affect each other, would lead to more canny and efficient diagnosis (and, as we'll see in Part Three, it brings other rewards too).

Our subject is the central dynamics of story—what makes it start, keeps it going, and determines its direction.

The cluster twinkles like a Disney Christmas with familiar, genial-seeming terms. But in fact it's a source of confusion, frustration, misconception, and miscarriage.

The confusion is betrayed initially by the cluster's disordered vocabulary. Ever since Aristotle first groped in its occulting gloom, commentators have failed to agree on a consistent lexicon: Philosophers, teachers, critics, and writers of how-to-write books have reinlessly used words like 'plot', 'story', 'structure', 'situation', 'theme', 'premise', 'proposition', 'conflict', 'opposition', 'jeopardy', 'point-of-attack', 'crisis', 'catharsis', 'resolution'— and on through an attic of jumbled and overlapping terminology.

Underlying this verbal pandemonium is, predictably, conceptual chaos: The words arise from ideas that are blurred and rimless.

This comes perilously close to saying that something essential to discuss is essentially undiscussable, but I have to bear-dance into it anyway because it's a crucial area that editors often mention, rarely think through, and never adequately understand, and my assignment is to make the case that something *can* be done about this.

We can start to close in on the subject with this broad notice: I'll be saying that the various forces and forms that create and direct vital motion in an orthodox story can be denoted with three words: 'character', 'situation', and what I'll temporarily call 'theme'.

Think of conflict, action, crisis, resolution, and similar eventualities not as narrative elements but as products of the elements.

Think of suspense, tension, interest, surprise, involvement, satisfaction not as being in the book at all but in the contemplator of the book—i.e., the reader—and that each can be traced back to a cause that *is* in the book.

Don't worry; I know what the voices in the back of the room are saying, but if we're going to communicate at all, we need to tolerate a tent-city cosmology and glossary of fiction while we survey this ancient battleground. There'll never be any final word on this subject, any more than there'll be one single book that contains everything doctors will ever want to know. Still, it's a subject that editors could learn more about with thought and study, and our industry should at least start work on the 'state of the craft' fiction-editing primer that will be revised in future editions as editors-to-come surpass us, which they certainly should.

Talk of character, situation, and theme hardly sounds new, but that's because the words aren't new. Whatever I say under them had better be new, if only because what *has* been available has been so contagiously muddled that he who would simply repeat it should be quarantined.

Those three denoting words designate a cluster so massive that to raise and exhibit it I'll sort it into two parts. Theme must wait for Part Three and the Notes. Character and situation are, I'll maintain, so bound together and interfused as to be a Siamese pair making up the soma of a novel, and I'll refer to them and all their parts as the *somacluster*.

Character. Since my emphasis will be on the *interplay* of the elements of the somacluster rather than a dissection of each, I'll dodge a lengthy segment by simply stipulating *character* to mean 'personal makeup', everything constant from the skin in. That a person is rich is not part of character, but that he's smart, callous, and bigoted is. That she's pregnant or has a terminal illness is situational rather than characterological, because it's not 'constant'.

Situation is comprised of two components: character *circuitry,* and *circumstance.*

Picture a snowbound mountain cabin inhabited by a pregnant woman approaching labor, and a man who is not the father. The man has with him a red attaché case with something in it that entails great jeopardy or opportunity.

Circuitry assumes the color and vibrance of individual characters; but it goes beyond to the chemistry, the electricity that runs between them—i.e., *how they affect each other.* The trip down that snowy mountain will be different for Clint Eastwood than it'll be for Woody Allen, but it will be further influenced by who goes down *with* him. Do the characters connect? Do they have conflicting vectors? Do they have overlapping fields of force at all? Answers to questions like these dictate the form and conductivity of the circuitry, the electrical wiring, of the cast of characters.

The elements forming *circumstance* include basic time-and-place, and *its* characterization, which is what's often called *setting.* If time-and-place may be thought of as background, the more dramatically useful elements of circumstance are the foreground, the *gads:* a dust storm (in Oklahoma in the thirties), a new eligible bachelor at Netherfield, an opening in a Cambridge college head-master's office, a man-eating shark offshore. A pregnancy coming to term next to a red attaché case in a blizzard. The notion of a *gad*, a stimulant, a spur, will be important in all this.

In some stories the precipitating tilt, the gadding force, comes primarily from the circumstance; in others it comes from the circuitry. In the most gripping ortho-dox fiction, all elements combine synergistically: Vital, driven, braided characters complement ingeniously a plunging Olympic slalom of circumstance, and we get hurtling, headlong drama.

Circumstantial gads—as in Oklahoma, Cambridge, and the others above—take the form of external threats and opportunities.

Successful circuitry requires gads too. Chemists refer to certain elements as 'inert', meaning that they only minimally combine or interact with other elements. Put them into an existent mixture, and nothing new and in-teresting happens. In fiction, inert characters can be a liability to narrative motion. The editor who has some understanding of the working of somaclusters will, when faced with a sluggish narrative, know how to examine each character and element of circumstance for its gad value. Remember, his assignment at this point is diagno-sis, which does not in itself prove anything; it merely refers the questions to sensibility: Could it be that the cause of the sluggishness is the inertness in this element?

It's critical to see that 'gad power' is not equivalent to sheer vitality. The question is whether the characters are right for each other. Think of a dinner party with

Caruso, Mao Tse-tung, and Hemingway. It's caviar, steak, and chocolate: separately, delights; simultaneously, garbage.

The first testing question about the circuitry-fit of a character is: Does he braid with other characters in the novel? The more fundamental question is: Does he braid *well*? Does this molecular structure and positioning make for optimal reaction, high current? In other words, does he provide fruitful gads and/or gad-receptors?

John Updike: "I was struck, talking to a biochemist friend of mine, how he emphasized not only the chemical composition of enzymes but their structure; it matters, among my humans, not only what they're made of but exactly how they attach to each other."

Joan Didion: "You have to make sure you have the characters you want. That's really the complicated part."

In different terms: What gad function does this character (shaped this way) serve? Does he spur other characters to characteristic action? (Adele is intellectual, proud, driven; her husband, Milt, is smooth, cunning, and weak; Jack happens on the scene; he is coarse, callous, humorous, smarter than Adele, stronger than Milt. We still have to devise the circumstance, but the circuitry is going in the right direction: The characters' strengths and foibles will serve as gads and gad-receptors for one another.) Granted, there are also other functions a character can serve—for example, connection or reflection—but the informed editor would know this too, he'd understand that the artist frequently has to make trade-offs. The point is to be canny enough to perceive when a trade-off is being made, which means being able to see distinct elements distinctly, and appreciate the possibilities of further bargaining.

Every student of fiction knows there's something to the notion of character circuitry. They've seen novels in which the principals are perfectly paired somehow, producing a special electricity in the air whenever they're in the same chamber. The student generalizes from this, suspecting that all pairing or ganging of characters can be more—or less—charged depending on how aptly interactive their chemistry, the orchestration, is.

In his good book *How Not to Write a Play,* Walter Kerr rightly decries the 'problem' play in which all the characters are whittled pawns trundling woodenly through the premises in the play's syllogism. Just take good, vital characters, says Kerr, put them on the stage, and let them generate their own heat, light, and motion. *But:* Kerr gives no advice on how *to select the right combination of characters* in the first place.

Shortly after Kerr's book was published, the Problem Play died, or was killed, by a play-form that had problems of its own. Osborne was Chekhov gone angry, and his best plays succeeded, as the problem plays of Ibsen did. But the form soon devolved to noisy still-lifes, and it was marked by the same internal ailments that afflict all fictions that begin solely with some flashy, articulate characters in situations that are drab, inert, without a motion-producing slope, with a circuitry that's circular indeed.

Circuitry can be faulty in several ways. We've focused on one: bad mix. And we've touched on another: excess characters, superfluities that can cause resistance, leaks, and short circuits in the system. The subtlest circuit problem of all—and it's one that many editors go a lifetime and never identify—is the missing character, a needed magnetic lode at or near the core, without which the neighboring wires are dormant, lacking current or harmonic vibrations. It's difficult to spot, but it will *never* be spotted if the editor isn't aware of it as a possible ailment and has no approach to diagnosing it.

If the effect of the snowbound narrative is totally compelling with just two characters, that is blessedly that. But if the effect is not all it might be, it would be immensely helpful if the editor were crafty enough to discern whether the optimal enrichment would come from an addition to character or to circuitry or to circumstance—or even to several of these.

The canny editor always starts diagnosis with symptoms, not rules for somaclusters. If, say, he's reading a novel about five people from the same hometown or college class, and sensibility notes that the thing seems to cough along with little sense of increasing momentum, just a rowboat surge and sag, he will immediately look for one of the usual causes of that symptom: a failure of circuitry because the lives never braid into one humming cable. The test exposes the fact that each life is separate from the others, and each time the author switches from one character to another, ignition is cut and the narrative RPMs drop toward zero. There have, of course, been successful novels with parallel but separate storylines that may finally come together only at the end. But if such a structure is successful, then diagnosis should never be applied, and its only allowable question—could *this* be the fault that needs remedy?—will never arise. (A hint about possible remedy comes from an observation about those novels that are successful despite multiple discrete storylines: See how often all the characters are reacting to the same general gad of circumstance.)

It's sometimes tempting to give solely the circuitry, and think the whole situation has been defined. "The situation is Ron is gay, and his boss, Ralph, hates gays." "The situation is a priest and a whore are isolated together." Situation must always include circumstance. "Ron's father owns the company." Can the priest and the whore leave their isolation at will? Are there pressures of external danger or opportunity? Is there a clock ticking? How Laura-the-klutz and Peter-the-mountain-climber interact depends on whether they're on Sutton Place or on an Alp.

All that seems obvious, but there's value in saying it out loud, because there is a tendency for the writer to be absorbed by the initial 'idea' with the cost of failing to develop early enough (or ever) the other necessary components of character and situation.

Let's move to the other half of situation: circumstance. If the how-to-write books agree on anything, it's on the necessity for an *issue,* something at stake. Even the portrait novel usually requires that the sitters have desires either to gain something or to preserve something. The novel of total ennui arose in France, and died some time ago, but even it had an issue—the desire for a desire. The issue was too vacuous, it was zero calories for the reader, no nourishment, no heat, and, like a celibacy cult, it was doomed.

In this essay I'm actively ruling meta-fiction out of consideration. My subject is the editing of novels of

orthodox narrative. *Ulysses* qualifies, so do fantasy novels, so long as they admit of identifiable emotions that
humans can partake of. The characters must feel pressure we can recognize. I've already argued that elements
of *circuitry* can impose pressures, and that's why they are
included under 'situation'. This isn't to say that the pressures of *circumstance* are restricted to inanimate forces like
forest fires and floods. For our purposes it isn't necessary
to define airtight scholastic categories of gads. An opportunity or threat arises. Sometimes its resolution will depend solely on the force of one personality on another,
and other times on a sheerly physical or solitary achievement. The important thing is that the gads be there, that
they be designed to lock-fit onto announced characterological aspects of principals, and that the reader also can
recognize and feel them. For the editor, the assignment
is to understand the essential craft of characterization,
circuitry, and circumstance so that if there is a weakness
he can detect what it is and promote repair.

Circumstance can be inadequate in different ways.
The editor's sensibility judges that it *is* inadequate, and
then it's the job of diagnosis to discern where and why.
It can be because the bolt of circumstance does not fit
tightly onto any latch of character. Or the gad can be
simply too small, too inconsequential. Or it can be nox-
ious, locking on to a motive that is despicable or narrowly
selfish. The most common problem is that the gad of
circumstance simply isn't urgent enough. This is when
the editor-physician's black bag must be reached for.

I should emphasize at once that though the black bag
must contain standard devices, 'devices' doesn't necessarily imply tiresome clichés. Read E. M. Forster on

devices, or ask a musicologist sometime to expound on the standard crafty devices that Beethoven used.

An example. The editor, faced with a congealing narrative, should ask himself if the cause of this lack of urgency may be the lack of a *time factor*. What's needed may be an impending deadline, even conflicting deadlines. The circumstance in the snowbound cabin has a built-in time factor that makes for a precipitating tilt: The pregnant woman is approaching labor. But can the circumstance of the red attaché case also be made to tick? The tilt increases. Can we make the two factors clash? (He *must* be at the top of the mountain; he *must* get her to the bottom.) More tilt. This needn't be cheap mustard disguising moldy beef. Character is most keenly revealed when it's confronted with crisis, hard choices, urgent decisions. Thus, insofar as he's interested in revealing character, the author's job is to construct circuitry and circumstance that will call for decisions, for actions. The sensible reader objects only when the circumstance and action feel synthetic, concocted, manipulated by the writer.

Consider: The situation on page one of every novel has been cunningly selected by the author and simply imposed on us. But because it has been assembled offstage, shielded from our judging eyes, it tends to be accepted more readily than a situation created right in front of us.

Another example. Picture Francine. Young, smart, with good impulses, but stuck in a barren, prejudiced western town in 1906. She's 'well drawn', we see her, hear her, appreciate her quirks and qualities, and we know what she wants: to escape her evangelist father and leave this town. But, curiously, as the pages begin to accumulate, the stasis of setting becomes stagnancy of narrative, and sympathy for Francine begins to turn to exasperation with her resourcelessness.

Maybe what Francine needs is a *plan.* She has a goal, but a goal alone can feel a flabby, passive thing. Have her adopt and announce to the reader a specific strategy for achieving the goal. *This is what I'm going to try. Here's how I'm going to get off the flat ground and onto a slope.* A plan frequently braces and tones up a sagging narrative. A plan entails an element of circumstance (or circuitry) that can be employed to advantage. Of course we can just wait for a traveling circumstance (salesman, lecturer, musician, sheriff) to arrive in town, but there is sometimes enlivening merit in having a Francine know from the outset, and design for herself, the method of her own salvation.

I'm not insisting that a scheme or crusade be mechanically revealed in the first eight minutes of every fiction. But notice how many playwrights from Shakespeare forward have designed not just the problem but an announced strategy into their opening scenes. (Shakespeare was as given to crafty devices as Beethoven was.) Sometimes a plan is the precise lift needed. The critical thing for the editor—and the writer—is simply to be aware of the tools at their command. If you don't need a ski lift at this moment, then don't go to it; if it is needed, it's comforting to know about it.

If the surface of a novel is jazzy, animated, and uproarious enough, the editor will seldom think to examine the circumstance beneath. He won't notice the murmured restiveness of sensibility. Here's a common error

of situation design. The familiar storyline has our heroine struggling to make it to the top. She arrives in New
York innocent and alone but bright, energetic, and
gifted. We see her ignored or abused as she sets forth on
her career, but through hard work, inspiration, and pluck
she defeats her enemies, survives her unworthy lovers,
and overcomes all obstacles at last to land the corner
office. The setup here seems perfectly recognizable and
adequate. Especially since it's so colorfully decorated
with the specific trappings of a setting or industry: We
learn fascinating things about how the television, maga-
zine, fashion, or cosmetics business really works. So it all
goes unquestioned by both author and editor.

And yet, when it's all over, something is missing.
That was okay, that story, I enjoyed it, lots of good stuff
in there. Not bad. And because it was "not bad", because
it didn't obviously fail, the editor doesn't rise to an explicit awareness of an insufficiency at the heart of things. He
doesn't say, "It held me, but it didn't seize me", and then
ask, "Why not?" If he did, again and again he'd find this
particular shortcoming in the familiar careerist story: Its
only goal is success, money, and power for the heroine—
but it would be so much more cherishable an endeavor
for her and for the reader if what were at stake included
a benefit for someone beyond just our protagonist. The
slope of narrative would be much sharper if the issue—
the situation she wants to arrive at—were not just her
coronation but the saving of the school, the operation for
the child, the acquittal of her unfairly accused dad. This
is not cliché; it's a fundamental rule of life and of fiction:
We feel greater gut-striving with anyone who is struggling for something more than just his own personal

gain. Granted: Some readers identifying with the heroine will have desires as self-centered as hers; their dream never includes triumph for a relative. Granted more: Sometimes the principle striven for is greater than personal pursuit, as when the black man in Mississippi fights for his rights as a human being. Granted again: The glitter of the scene, the wit of the heroine, the loathsomeness of the opposition can combine into a read of such jamboree that the editor never notices his sensibility asking: Yes, but should it have been still better? Was the narrative as widely and deeply compelling as it should have been?

Another diagnostic question that may point to a somacluster problem: Is the narrative too austerely narrow, too bony-lean and singular? Of course that's exactly where the greatness lies in some novels and plays. But others that we can all recall have been rounded and enriched by counterpoints and subplots that we'd now be horrified to see cut out. The great chef will sometimes serve up his main course in regal solitude; there it is, nothing *on* it and nothing *near* it. But other times he realizes its best qualities will be brought out only by an accompanying taste. Sensibility is the arbiter, but the editor must be trained enough to recognize when complication is called for.

And he must have at his fingertips a range of complications. Give Joel a conflict within himself. Or have Jaime bent on destroying Joel. Or have Jaime indifferent toward Joel except he wants the same piece of land, or a different use for it. Or even consider blind conflict: An abduction team closes in on its prey, unaware that an assassination team is approaching the prey from another direction entirely.

At the heart of circumstance are its gads. What is *not* a gad should be minimalized or eliminated entirely. "Select!" say the writing books, and never give clear advice about how to approach that task. 'Theme' aside, the needs of an efficient and effective somacluster are the best guides. The astute historical novelist knows the danger of his research: He may cram circumstance with gadless data. A gad must come with sufficient information so that we know why it is a gad and to whom, but the editor must be alert to when furnishing has become clutter. This isn't always easy, but the good sensibility will recognize when the extensive description of bric-a-brac is necessary if we are to feel why Maud loves her mansion, and when it's just garrulous, encumbering accumulation.

Hollywood and Broadway, at their approvable best, have always been more keenly alert to story failings than Publishers' Row. They turn away from novels in which the issue is: Why did Henry break the teacup? They are wary of *sagas*—the narratives spanning a couple of generations. They are sometimes wrong about this, but when they see lines like, "Two years later . . .", "Eight years passed . . ." it means to them that there's obviously no ongoing problem of high temperature. We parody them by depicting a twenty-six-year-old studio chief with dark green glasses yammering through a clenched cigar, "Where's the jeopardy!? What's the twist?" and we say, Ah, well, that's Hollywood.

If the pursuit of the picaresque is the vice of the superficial (as Melvin Seiden said), then Hollywood at its worst is one end of a spectrum: bonging clocks; wild-eyed, director-crazed horses hopping like puppies; 'production values' brocading miles of celluloid into pizza (Bankhead said of Maeterlinck: "There is less to this than meets the eye."); action frantically fisted on like vindicating ketchup. You've read the comic strip, now see the movie. But at the other end of that spectrum there are books, lots of them, with no jeopardy, twists, clocks, horses, production values, or ketchup at all. Some of these nevertheless achieve wondrously a satisfying rightness, while many more are stillborn, prematurely ripped forth, somatically undeveloped. A good editor might have saved some. In calling for more editorial performance, I don't worry about a flu of publishing megos in green glasses ordering up a horse with ketchup on it.

There are two pertinent features that distinguish our industry from Hollywood, and the happy first is: When it comes to the final script, the writer is the boss. The second is: If ever it were the case that what the script needs is a spicy stallion, it's unlikely that anyone on editorial row would consistently know it.

I've talked about elements within the somacluster—circuitry, circumstance, setting, gads—and the desirability of being able to apply a systematic medical checkup to a given element to see if, possibly, it's what's causing a certain undesirable reaction in the reader. What would such a systematic procedure look like? For an example, let's focus on a key element in the cluster: character. The tool I'll describe is the *character grid*.

The character grid is distinguished from the *character profile*. The profile is an aid to 'characterization'—that is, the various ways in which a writer 'brings his people to life' by making the reader see, hear, and feel them.

Those writers who find it helpful to work up character profiles may use an identity questionnaire, starting with basic data like birthplace, appearance, education, and employment, up through hobbies, what the character reads, what makes him angry or ashamed or relaxed, what makes him laugh, what his deepest secret is, what he does on Thursday nights and Sunday afternoons. Earlier I said that the question of circuitry takes for granted the color, the vibrance, the profile of the character. So does the grid. What the grid is looking at is the 'story value' of the character.

Suppose sensibility registers that something is not right with Ben in the story. Oh, he's vivid enough, and he feels authentic; he doesn't disappear for long stretches or do incredible things. But still sensibility has suspicions. What might be wrong with him?

Put his name on the left-hand side of a piece of paper, and across the top write these questions:

- *What does he want or promise?*
- *What does he do to make it happen?*
- *What effect does he have?*
- *Do we care strongly for (or against) him as a person?*
- *Do we care about his goal?*
- *Does he braid or conflict with others in the cast?* (This, of course, is a question about circuitry—which would have its own tests, for how *well* he braids or conflicts. It would examine personal gads and gad-receptors, and

how often plugs make contact with sockets, causing current to flow.)

- *Is he 'resolved'?*

The first question can be restated: What in his situation—his circuitry or circumstance—does he want to change or save from change? (Or what impact does he threaten to have, regardless of wanting it—like, say, Typhoid Mary?)

So the third question can be rephrased to ask: *Do* his acts change circuitry or situation?

'Resolution', in these terms, means: Does he either change the situation or have his attitude toward it changed? (Or have his threat/promise defused, or detonated?)

Don't demand that each query be matched by a ringing answer that would bring game-show applause from the College of Cardinals, but know that if there are enough negative answers to these queries, there's a chance that the trouble with vivid, believable Ben is that he doesn't belong in the book at all.

One of the values of this coldly clinical grid is this: If Ben is loud, bright, and ubiquitous enough, his stage-center posture may deflect us from ever entertaining the notion that, as currently endowed, he may be superfluous. We won't even *ask* if he goes after anything or affects another character. But a character can be loud and ubiquitous and still be a drag on the novel's momentum. The grid forces us to review Ben.

And the character grid can ensure that we don't overlook the flaw in the eleven-year-old boy who plays with matches. He's a minor figure in the book, but he can qualify as a lesser lesion if he goes undiagnosed because, in the emergency-room heat, the editor confines all his attention to arresting the blatant hemorrhages. The first question in the character grid would start to focus right on the ailment in the boy. He promises a flaming crisis. He doesn't deliver. Craft would ensure that even minor internals such as this are treated.

In sum, the grid is designed to detect two generic failures in character. Either the character is profiled okay but his promise or potential is not fulfilled, or the character had no justifiable function in the first place. Keep him, but make him pay his dues, or kick him out.

I should quickly say several things. The first is to repeat that craft *proves* nothing. It's only an aid to sensibility in identifying the culprit if there is one. Jordan Baker in *The Great Gatsby* would pull a 'no' to six of the seven grid questions. And sensibility would say, "I don't care; she's fine and the book's fine. Get away from it with that grid." (The one she gets a 'yes' on saves her; she *does* braid, with Nick, and with the Buchanans, making a needed fourth. She's not a gad, she's a connection, but a necessary one, as tendon is to muscle. It's also true that she fits and contributes in another way: She allegedly cheats at golf, but Nick accepts her anyway, which promotes Fitzgerald's aim of conveying Nick as a non-judgmental man.)

It's true that if you wrote the whole roster of major characters down that left-hand column, and the cross-boxes all came up negative, I'd bet you'd have a dreary reading experience on your hands. But it's not dreary because it fails the grid; both the flunk *and* the dreariness are caused by flaws in the novel—weakness of circuitry, lack of compelling gads, driveless characters, and so no slope, no motion.

In the end, Senior Editor may look at the grids, rosters, and checklists and say, "Well, that's just not my style." The style here is one of learning and applying craft, and ensuring that the craft entails systematic analysis that makes for depth and thoroughness. To which Senior Editor replies, "Well, there are systems and there are systems. He has his, I have mine. You ask one of my authors, who's got one of my twenty-page letters, if I'm thorough or not."

Answer: Yes, the author will think he's thorough. Not one author in ten will complain that an editor hasn't found enough wrong in his script. Except for those few authors who knowingly submit shabby first drafts, writers tend to believe that what they finally hand in is pretty good, the result of—among other things—care and hard work. Thus *any* catches by the editor will startle them. "Lord, I never noticed that, and I rewrote that scene eight times! How clever you are!" We *want* our editor to be smart, just as we do our coach or doctor. Smart and thorough. But consider: If the editor, coach, doctor were *not* informed and thorough, how would the client know?

Senior Editor's careful line-to-line editing (his 'system') may produce hundreds of detail corrections, and the author is awed. "Is he thorough!? The tiniest pimple doesn't escape him!" He is awed—and he is undertreated.

Picture the city building inspector strolling through the rubble of a collapsed hotel. "How we going to figure this out, Ed?" asks his assistant. "Shall we check the architect's designs? The jointing technique? The strength of the steel supports?" "There are systems and there are systems," says Ed thoughtfully. "My strolling system is good. Look at this here gargoyle. Is that ugly or is it hideous, which? Ho! Wait'll you see the length of the report I produce."

There *are* systems and systems, and there are styles and styles. But my categorical position is that some are inadequate for a given job. There are no necessary rules for the artist. The architect can envision what he likes. But if his buildings keep falling down, the structural engineer's advice is needed, and he must bring with him disciplined, thorough systems of diagnosis, with checklists of questions and qualitative-analysis tests for the answers. Unsystematic diagnosis is notorious for missing the second ailment: The patient with abdominal pain is treated for a perforated ulcer, only to die from a simultaneous ruptured appendix. It's not good enough in engineering, in medicine, or in editing.

Of course there are editors now practicing who will comment on 'characterization', 'motivation', 'conflict'. And they're often aware when a fictional persona is a failure because it's drab, aimless, unlovable, unbelievable, two-dimensional, with the weight and palette of Kleenex. Authors will give testimonials that their editors have nailed them with a basic diagnosis. ("We're supposed to like Ingrid, but she comes across as a whiner.") And that they've even spotted failures of circuitry by collaring nonessential loiterers on the scene. These sporadic insights are worth having, but just as editors can 'know about' point of view and miss all but the most obvious blunders, they can patrol their texts for a whole career and never once discern the need for an additional subplot. Their instincts may sometimes look like magic. I'm in favor of instinct, and I love magic shows. But I want someone who can go beyond his few special tricks.

Like Conan Doyle's great teacher at medical school, an editor can sometimes spot the symptom and the cause from across the room. But when the proud doctor (or his ectype, Sherlock Holmes) could not, he resorted to technology. There is, at least theoretically, a set of codifiable analytic tools that will provide a workup on the basic components of orthodox narrative (not Borges or Barthelme).

I should repeat the caveat at various intervals: The function of craft is to diagnose. It does not evaluate. Sensibility does that. Though I'll say this again and again, I realize that in emphasizing the craft of editing I risk appearing to be an engineer trying to assay poetry with a Geiger counter. But, always, my premise is that response comes first; all diagnostic craft can do is point out *possible* spoilers in the test; it rounds up likely suspects. Sensibility must address the police lineup and say yes, that's the villain, or, no, none of these. Or say there is no villain; everything is okay. It's important that sensibility always have the deciding vote. If two consecutive four-syllable words *work,* leave them alone; if the truth is that you aren't bothered by the fact that Nick's actions make no difference, then pass on. Craft can only ask: "Is this it?" Craft can never say this must be it.

Agreed: The danger of craft is that it induces foolish slavishness. This is true in would-be artists, and in editors of manic industry and no sense.

If an approach that utilizes such things as 'grids' seems too mechanical, too confining, too much removed from the unregimentable thing we all feel art to be, it's probably because I haven't convinced you these tools aren't meant to be procedural formulas for how to write, or tests for proving that a book must be defective.

It's *sensibility* that registers disappointment when Cora at the end elects to go off with Andrew. Why? "Well, he's not a bad guy, really." Then why? "Well . . . I guess because he feels like such a *lightweight.*" Why? The grid suggests why: He wants nothing much, he *does* nothing at all. No effect. No impact. No weight. At this point it's still up to sensibility to judge if that's the cause. (It *might* be caused by facets of characterization—his appearance, the way he always hides his hands in his armpits like a child, his passion for mah-jongg.)

I emphasize that the suppressed premise of a grid is not "This is what the novel should do." But I'd look suspiciously disingenuous if I didn't acknowledge that some writers do use methodical tools like this as they compose. I have seen startlingly elaborate charts, graphs, timetables, and critical-path diagrams that novelists have devised to help them keep track of the mercurial flows of story.

Don't think such authors must be mechanical hacks. One of the most subtle, dramatic, and moving novels I ever published had been planned by the author in a blackboard-sized diagram using eight different-colored pencils. He needed it to help him shape and control the changing patterns of character, circuitry, and circumstance. If it worked for him, I'm glad he had it. If he'd ever asked me to display similar tracking tools that others had used, I'd have been glad to display them. But at no time would I ever have said, "You *must* use this." I *would* tell an editor, "You must use this or something very like it, otherwise you'll get lost in that book." (I would say this only to an editor with the intellect, industry, and temperament to accept it. To have the temperament he probably has to be young. In publishing, the satellites of art become fixed early in a firm, undeviating path. Editors, like benighted medieval minions, pass quickly into confident rigidity.)

None of this means to assert that a productive soma-cluster, dense profile, positive grid, plus well-chosen POV equals good novel. If the writer does not have the artistry described in Part Three, the novel will be paste and plastic. Good form only allows it to get done; it doesn't *do* it.

Don't apply the character grid for orthodox narrative fiction to *Catcher in the Rye.* Sensibility (for Salinger's ideal intended audience and the aptly responding editor) says that book is *well.* Therapy can only harm it. (I know there are critics who would have that book different, but it's a novel that pleased and awed a generation, so such a critic, while entitled to his own view, would be wrong as the editor for the book.) Don't ask short stories—especially good *New Yorker* stories—to satisfy the grids. The response they're looking for is different from that of a novel, and they often effect the cherishable thing superbly.

There will always be readers whose first appetite is to find evident exceptions ("Show me how your character grid would work on *The Sound and the Fury!*"), not to test the limits of a tool, but to disqualify it entirely. Don't do that. Realize that no book, person, or multiplicitous thesis will ever be perfect. The motive that simply yearns to be able to sneer the whole thing away is an impoverishing one; I know because I've seen myself do it and, after reflection, I realized that not only was I not larger by having taken in the good fraction of what I rejected, I was actually smaller in the way that our small acts make us. If there were a good textbook of craft, I promise I would hug it to me and press copies on my colleagues. If ever you reach the point where you are convinced no one knows anything worthwhile that you don't, or where you feel no rush at the prospect of encountering someone who could teach you new things in your work, the top layer of your brain has died.

I'll conclude Part Two by restating the convictions behind my plea for craft: It's possible to respond aptly to a novel without being able to identify what's causing that response. If it's a negative response, we can devise valid systematic techniques for diagnosing at least some of the ailments that sensibility has registered. To deny this in defense of art is to misunderstand the editor's task, and to deny craft altogether. And without craft, the work of the editor will forever be fitful, shallow, and incomplete.

REVISION
AND
ART

We're now two-thirds of the way through the editor's agenda. He's read and reacted; he's identified (with a greater or lesser specificity) the causes of his reactions. The first phase took sensibility; the second, sensibility plus craft. The third phase is revision, and it calls for sensibility, craft, and art.

Art? From an editor? Yes, a part of it. A small, not only possible but necessary part.

To explain this, I'll need to examine, however conjecturally, the act of art. For this risky business, we need a common understanding of certain prior concepts, and we can start with a closer look at sensibility.

There are two kinds of sensibility.

The first is the one that tastes and judges; it's a taste-bud performance; call it *gustant*.

The second is the one that registers, among other things, appetite, anticipation, anxiety, curiosity. It too is responsive, the way any craving is. Call it *salivant*.

All revisions are aimed at correcting what's already there, or supplying needed things that are missing, so they'll be either cuts or additions or (a combination of the two) changes.

Calls for revision could originate with reactions by either one of the two sensibilities. For example, gustant sensibility tends to initiate most cuts: "Delete? It's not funny." Or, "It's not believable, and it doesn't contribute." Or, "It feels repetitious." Or, "It's not interesting enough to compensate for how much it's slowing things up."

Salivant sensibility tends to be the dominant impulse behind requests for additions—as when the editor/reader turns the last page of a murder mystery and finds that the author never tells whodunit. But salivancy can respond to things much more subtle than that, and at its most advanced point it can bring the editor to the very edge of art.

Art is an awesome, animate, unreasonable main at the far end of which there's no boundary that I can see, but at this end it laps tamely on the beach of craft—sometimes, over generations, even washing up new permanent strands on the island of technique. The best editor can be asked to go wading, hugging the shore where its slope is gradual, and he can always touch bottom. But, wading, hugging, touching, he is still at the eerie littoral of the great act itself.

We'll get back to each of these notions of sensibility, and how they play into the work of revision, after we examine something of what goes on in an act of art.

Every act of art parses into three stages. I won't, in this anatomizing, count the original conceiving of the book itself. The editor *is* sometimes involved in helping the author find or evaluate his next book idea, and this immensely important assignment must be addressed (see *Initia* in the Notes), but for the moment I'll restrict myself to the labor required once the novel is under way.

That has to be said because many writers won't readily recognize their work as breaking into the three stages

I define. In particular will the first stage seem unrecognizable if they think I'm talking about how they got the initial notions for the novel. The 'act of art' that I'll be referring to assumes a work is already conceived, however inchoately. It also implies that the creation of large scenes, characters, predicaments, events entails a *series* of acts of art and, indeed, that the selections of individual phrases and words are discretely artful. Momentarily picture the writer already at work. He's in the middle of a page and is now grappling with the question of what comes next. It's going to come out of his head. What goes on *in* his head will be an act of art.

The first stage of a creative act is a sensation for which we have no single word in English, but which we all recognize, and it is: a longing or craving or appetite *the specific satisfier of which is not yet named.* Imagine a cook sampling a soup in progress. Cook, squinting, says, *"Needs* something! Let's see now . . ."

Notice that the immediate sensation—call it the *prelibation* ('foretaste') is in terms of effect on the consumer's palate. "I want it to have this flavor, impact, satisfaction." "I need something here that will start the reader liking Jenny and rooting for her." "I need an adjective to convey what her smile was like." "It has to feel as if Paul is truly settled now, all anxiety is past." "I have to start building an atmosphere of menace in the castle." "It's time for the confrontation between Bart and Erica." (Over these few paragraphs, keep clear in your mind the difference between the *effect*—the impact, tease, mood, tension, build, relief, satisfaction—and *the narrative that effects it.*)

This palatal craving triggers the second stage in the

art act: *Imagination,* nudged by the yearning prelibation, comes up with ingredients it says will do the trick. (Jenny can sell her ring so she can give Celia the money for the trip.) (Her smile was 'cold'? 'gelid'? *'reptilian'!*) Thus the craving can last for a fraction of a second or for weeks. Sometimes it's satisfied so quickly—as, for example, when we reach for the right word—that the mind can't distinguish between the thought and the word the thought summons up (inclining certain philosophers to maintain, wrongly, that we think in words.)

As a flexible and focused imagination serves up its menu, the third stage of art begins: *Sensibility* tastes the offering intended to achieve the effect, and it says, "Yes, that does it," or "No, not quite right." (No to 'cold', no to 'gelid', yes to 'reptilian'.) If it's not right, what often ensues is a slightly more pointed and articulate aware-ness of the feeling that's wanted, and the imagination goes back to work, closer to target.

Those are the three stages of artful writing: *preliba-tion, imagination, selection.*

For some writers, the narrative seems to flow out of their hands with such easeful instinct they're unaware of any premeditation. But the majority—and among them some of the greatest writers whose testimony has been available—talk of the frequent struggle to find the im-ages and actions (and the words to express them) that will be the 'objective correlative' for the effect they are bent on. This prelibation, the anticipation of the *effect,* is clear, unmistakable, urgent—and now imagination must produce the specific satisfying narrative.

I use the word 'narrative' here to mean the lamina-tion of things imagined and the words used to describe them. The artist imagines his specific scene and, in a parallel act of art, conjures the words that will convey it. This real distinction is not advanced in the most famous single sentence ever written on the general matter, Eliot's line about the 'objective correlative': "The only way of expressing emotion in the form of art is by finding an 'objective correlative'; in other words, a set of objects, a situation, a chain of events which shall be the formula of that *particular* emotion; such that when the external facts, which must terminate in sensory experience, are given, the emotion is immediately evoked." That Eliot does not mention the difference between the external facts and the words needed to convey them is not sufficient reason to believe he didn't see it; I suspect he did, but also decided to unite the two because the difference was irrelevant to his point.

It's clear he *did* see the distinction between an awareness of the effect wanted (the evoking of a particular "emotion") and an intuition of the narrative that will produce it. It's possible to have a prelibation with no idea of what narrative would fulfill it.

We tend to think of art as solely imagination, fecundity of fancy. But experienced editors have again and again seen its three aspects discrete, the most common and vivid demonstration of their discreteness coming in the writers who show huge inventiveness and no sensibility whatever. A subtler, more profound manifestation is seen in writers who have adequate imagination and sensibility of a sort, but who seem curiously deaf to what the reader craves to hear about.

That *something*—prelibation—always prompts and channels imagination seems obvious when we think about it. Imagination's potential offerings are as count-less as the atoms. But in fact the creating mind is not constantly deluged with an ocean of random imaginings. Yes, writers will sometimes claim, "I'm not nearly as deliberate as all that sounds. My stuff just comes to me!" It may feel this way, but when the writer is on page ninety-nine of his novel about Henry VIII, it does not "come to him" to start page one hundred with an excit-ing car chase through Chicago. Though his imagination is capable of conjuring up Chicago, it does not at this point do so, nor does it usher forth a Viking ship, a rock star backstage, a child playing with a live panda bear, all of which it *could* produce—because prelibation is at work, prompting and restricting.

Don't feel that this parsing of art is an attempt to demystify it. By citing and celebrating prelibation as equally important with the imagination and sensibility, I'm suggesting that art is even more complexly wondrous than some of us thought it was.

Indeed, I sometimes think that we're closer to the mysterious heart of art when we study not the *imagination* but the *prelibation*: It's impressive to see an author sum-mon up the precise protein, vitamin, or condiment that the narrative could use right here, but it's often more awesome *that it occurred to him that anything was needed at all.*

Orwell, intending keen approval, once wrote: "The outstanding, unmistakable mark of Dickens's writing is the *unnecessary detail.*" Orwell's emphasis would occur only to an admiring savant of the art. And he did mean it as admiration—the details he cites are triumphs. It's the fact that they are "unnecessary" that makes them stupendous, that prompts the expert to gasp, "What made him think of it!?" Yes, his imagination did the work, it found the ingredient; but, even before that, what told him there was effective work that could be done, that a flavor of a certain kind would be delightful right here?

If we can agree that there is such a thing as prelibation in the artist, Orwell's remark leads us to the next observation: There are two kinds of prelibation—implied and unimplied.

Virginia Woolf praised Jane Austen for never failing to supply the 'obligatory scene'. Woolf did not mean some sort of technical obligation like those entailed in sonnets or haiku. She meant that Austen always knew what appetite, what fear—what *salivancy*—was building up in the reader, and she consummated it.

Implied prelibations are those longings-for-an-effect that the author feels and that are so directly a teased product of what has gone before in the novel that the reader too is conscious of anticipation, of wanting, of curiosity, of hoping or fearing—of salivancy. When the effect is all but mandatory, the fulfillment of a clear promise or responsibility, the prelibation—the sense of the need for the effect—is implied.

They include a yearning to know what's in that locked tower, who killed his lordship and how, why the mother had a breakdown, what will happen to the inheritance. They call for confrontation between betrayer and betrayed, for comeuppance to the villain, for conflagrations, exposés, confessions, beddings-down. We must be given the battle scene, the final race, the revolution, the breakthrough. We must see the quiet man, pressed too far, rise to the challenge, the abused woman come to her senses, the matriarch realize at last what she has done.

What we deserve is not all happy endings, but endings certain, completions, consummations. Why must we be given these things? Because with hint, tease, the building of unresolved chords, the aromas from the kitchen—we have been promised them.

*Un*implied prelibations in the author make up the vast majority of his intuitions of what effect should come next. They are much the more magical kind of prelibation. They include Orwell's 'unnecessary details'. The awareness that you have to satisfy the reader-salivancy to know what happened to that ticking bomb is so basic an intuition as hardly to deserve the name of artistry.

What qualifies a prelibation as unimplied is the fact that it's not patently indicated by what has gone before; it's not something that the common reader would demand or expect. But something within the author does demand it.

A genus of unimplied prelibation that all authors will recognize is the need for 'prepping', the *positioning* of the reader's sensibility for a later impact. ("If I make the reader distrust Jonas right here, it will be tastier later on when I . . .").

Another genus could be called unimplied corroboration. *Implied* corroboration is the familiar 'showing rather than telling' that editors often ask for: Don't just *assert* that Sally is funny and smart—depict her being so. Unimplied corroborations are inspired, quirky details of character, scene, or action that vivify the narrative in ways no editor would have dreamed of.

Still another genus is the craving for a certain meaningful modulation that prompted Hemingway to imagine the fishing scene in *The Sun Also Rises;* Tolstoi to send

Levin out for a whole chapter just to reap wheat; Melville to ask, "How can I hope to explain myself here?" and yet to know that "in some dim, random way, explain myself I must, else all these chapters might be naught," and then indite his fearsome, magniloquent passage on 'The Whiteness of the Whale'; or Shakespeare to trouble forth his witches in *Macbeth*—all episodes that, by any artlessly mechanical measure such as "everything must advance the story", would be deleted, at immense aesthetic loss.

That last—a sense of the felicitousness of modulation at this point, a change of pace, a new color, a new instrument in solo (but always with a contributing narrative value too)—suggests another way of conveying how the writer's salivant sensibility goes beyond that of the reader: Where the reader may be said to be confined to prelibations of *appetite,* the writer can sense that and more: He can sense *readiness.* An unmistakable sign of an unimplied prelibation (that the author has felt) is when the reader is surprised. If the surprise is what we'd call a good one (not necessarily good news, but to good effect) we have to credit not only the writer's imagination, which conjured the specific event, but the prelibation, his intuition that the reader's sensibility was ready for just this effect. In life, a surprise gift to us usually delights, but a surprise gift of a species that would never have occurred even to us and which brings great, never-anticipated pleasure—this takes us beyond delight to bewitchment. The best writers are good witches.

Unimplied prelibation stirs continually in the writer: Every word, every scene, every single element in a novel is ushered in by prelibation, and very little is mandatory. It's this inspired stream of seemingly unprompted intuitions of what next effect would be great right here that I claim is at the heart of art as much as imagination is. But in the same way as imagination is guided and restricted by prelibation, prelibations themselves are also channeled. When the cues are so loud even the reader can hear them, the prelibations are implied. One of the mysteries of the artist's mind is that he is hearing things the rest of us can't; his seismic intuition is sensing flows and thrustings long before they reach the surface. His next scene may be "seemingly unprompted" even to him, but it is not unprompted, and the unimplied prelibation that causes it is itself a response: Everything that has come before in his novel, whatever vision he has of what is yet to come, and his desire for a larger-scale effect, within which this scene is only one factor—all these things are acting on him, whispering at him, issuing an aesthetic command: And now *this!* The 'this' is an effect-wanted, which in turn commands imagination. Writers are not the only artists who testify to this; musicians, dancers, even architects will describe how the flow of what they've done up to this point has built a craving for a certain continuation, or a culminating effect, and that their first awareness is of a *feeling* they want here, and only subsequently do they imagine the specific elements that will produce it.

There's an argument that the distinction between implied and unimplied prelibation is only a matter of degree—indeed, close-reading and perceptive critics have often sought to show how unexpected developments in a novel were 'inevitable'. And certainly we've all noticed that while some spectators are shocked by a given turn of events, others can say with sincerity, "I knew that was going to happen." The argument is not wrong but it is weak, I think, at the most interesting level of art. We've all read poets' strokes of such unexpected inspiration that to detect their origins would take eyes that can see atoms unaided.

Now, with this rickety schema of art trembling in place, we can get back to the two kinds of sensibility, how they play into revision, and how the editor, by going ankle-deep into art himself, might contribute to correction of what is already written and even help the author to find his way to new waters entirely.

Almost universally, the editor's efforts at the stage of revision are confined to promoting two things:

- *Elimination of insults to gustant sensibility.*
- *Remedy of disappointments to salivant sensibility.*

His requests for these two will usually be simple extensions of the articulations of diagnosis.

I have skimped the act of articulation, but in fact it obtains at each stage of editing. The editor reads, responds, and more or less articulates his response: "I don't like Jane, so I can't care about what she wants." If the response is negative, diagnosis pinpoints the cause, and he articulates it: "I don't like her because she strangles the puppy." This last is tantamount to an articulation of a needed repair: "Have Jane not strangle the puppy." Clear and pertinent articulations are one of the yields of good diagnosis.

If Jane has killed Puppy in frustrated reaction to something having nothing to do with the animal, simply deleting the event may be sufficient medicine to soothe

the upset gustant sensibility. But if she has killed Puppy because he has whined all night, her performance is both disgusting and disappointing. Which means that the editor/reader has had both a gustant and a salivant response: He doesn't like what he does see, and he has had a hope, however vague ("Help the puppy!"), dashed. (It's certainly true that an author may be 'right' in disappointing the reader on occasion because a larger, longer-term effect is enhanced; the point is not that the readers should always be fed their immediate candy, but if the current bitterness is shown by book's end to overbalance—indeed, to defeat—ultimate satisfaction, the author should be told.) In the case of the unhappily whining pup, a laconic instruction from the director's chair to "cut the strangulation" is not sufficient. That still leaves the yearning (for first aid to Puppy) that the author has stimulated. Strictly, only gustancy judges; salivancy does not, since it simply anticipates. When salivancy is disappointed, the subsequent bad feeling is gustant. In any case, the model editor proceeds methodically through his diagnostic notes, converting them into suggested treatment.

When the problem is salivant, the remedy usually comes down to either cutting the stimulus or fulfilling it. Diagnosis and treatment of this kind is worthwhile even if the narrative wen is so small as to be subliminal in effect. It's an accepted minor rule of craft that a writer should not mention the name of a character if it serves no immediate function and he'll never reappear: "Ralph asked the barman, Joe Harkness, for a double scotch." Delete 'Joe Harkness'. Analogously: "He paid for it with a five-dollar bill and took three quarters in change." Unless, say, he'll soon tell someone he can't lend a quarter because he has none, the line should be deleted, because it excites a suspicion of pertinence, an expectation, however sotto voce, in the reader. The writer—or editor— who leaves it in, on the principle that the accumulation of any detail is what makes a scene rich and realistic, shows an imperfect sensibility—both gustant and salivant. In fiction, a fact is not necessarily a factor. (The brilliant 'unnecessary' detail is not brilliant if it brings with it a promise that is not thereafter fulfilled.)

I have withheld from this essay a discussion of the varying degrees of *specificity* that editors achieve as they make their recommendations for cuts, changes, and additions. I've done this in part because it inevitably entails a long look at imagination, which, I would find myself arguing, is *also* not a single, one-step, homogeneous event. The argument is intricate, and probably tedious. I can skip it because my position is that prelibation is as far into art as we can expect the editor to go, both because it requires a special talent to go further and because, even if he had that talent, most authors want their editors to be editors and not co-writers.

We can sum up the editor's usual performance during revision by saying that, having articulated the diagnoses that cries of gustant and salivant sensibility evoke, he converts the analyses into suggestions for specific cuts, changes, and additions. It's routine editorial work: All it requires is intelligence, sensitivity, tact, articulateness, industry, patience, accessibility, promptness, orderliness, thoroughness, a capacity to work alone, a capacity to work with others. Plus sensibility and craft. No humans need apply.

In asking him to do this job, to read and respond

aptly, to apply an array of diagnostic tools that are expert, methodical, and flexible enough to allow him to
range over and check each component of the dermal and
internal systems embodying orthodox narrative fiction,
to be exhaustive, non-rambling, non-ambiguous and
non-vague in his prescriptions, and at the last, to go
beyond the clamors of gustancy to the keen pleas of
salivancy, we are, finally, asking him to wade the sea-edge
surf of art itself. Salivancy is at the heart of implied prelibation, and prelibation is the first moment in the act of
art.

But if such an editing paragon did exist, even at his
best there are depths that would be beyond him. It's true
that, wading on the strand, an editor with a superbly
responsive sensibility has been known to call for a new
character or a valuable modulation. But when he does
this, it's almost always in reaction to a subtle faltering in
the manuscript. (He senses a void in the heroine's world;
she must have *some* close friend, or maybe a sister. He
feels a reader's restive curiosity about what a character
does on his day off or what he does for, or instead of, sex.
Or he registers a satiation with action, or its opposite,
and he calls for a change of pace.) This work is rare and
commendable, but, still, it's retroactive; after the desirable element has not been provided, he misses it. Certainly authors do this too. But what gifted authors also do
that an editor does not is foresee the enriching effect of
a new character or scene whose absence would originally
never have been noted even retroactively, but whose
presence we prize and marvel at, and which moves us to
say again: "What made him think of it!" I can't think of
any training, craft, grid, or analysis that would enable the

editor himself to prelibate the effect of a new character, accident, death, or departure of the kind I've been calling unimplied. Never mind his then imagining the narrative that executes. The greatest inventions of fiction cruise farther out than any editor's horizon, and deeper than he could ever sound. To these submerged canyons, where The White Whale and Falstaff were spawned, and Gatsby conceived his party, and The Bear first roamed, no editor goes.

Which is why I say that the editor's contribution at the revision stage almost always stops with his attention to the demands of gustant and salivant sensibility.

But, just theoretically, he could, on rare occasion, help a writer to find his own way to those unfathomable seabeds where the most mysterious and oceanic art arises.

This effort by the editor makes undisguisable the shift in his focus. He is moving from the *written* toward the *act of writing,* and there is peril here, from both its effect and its reception. To start with an example of a tip that is small and acceptably benign, consider the problem known as 'writer's block'.

Writer's block is not a failure of imagination; it's a failure of prelibation. Imagination has not died during writer's block; it has simply gone still from lack of instruction. The type we'll consider is midstream block. Assume the writer is well into his novel when he suddenly goes dry. Nothing comes to him when he asks, "And now what?" Day after day he stares at a blank page. Moved to help, the good editor who has a rudimentary grasp of the act of art might look for a way to stimulate the writer's prelibation, and his method emerges from a realization that prelibation arises not just out of a vision of what the rest of the novel should be, but out of what has already been written, from the opening somacluster—the initial setup of character, circuitry and circumstance—and the events these precipitate, and the subsequent, reshaped somacluster the events have caused. Each new development of character, circuitry, circumstance, or POV stirs prelibation and prompts the "And now *this!*" that is the motor of narrative. (Many writers totally count on this, seldom knowing what their ending will be until they get there.) So the editor's prescription is: *Go back and change a basic element.* Alter the banks of the stream of narrative to arrive back at today's page with a river of different currents, cataracts, and volume roaring into the resistant gulch. There's a good chance that new prelibation will open up.

The editor's therapeutic technique becomes more fraught with misgiving when he addresses the ostensible opposite of block, writer's hyperemia. The problem here isn't that the writer can't think of anything to come next; it's that each day he fills pages and at the end of the week he sees they're all 'irrelevant' and have to be thrown out. His difficulty is not that he has *no* prelibations; it's that he has too many; they come on without control, like jabbered schizoid bursts. But at base the hyperemic author's complaint is the same as the blocked: He doesn't know what should come next.

If the problem behind midstream *block* lies in the somacluster, a still further problem, and the one certainly behind *hyperemia,* is the second of those two forces that I named as directing and driving fiction narrative. The first was somacluster itself. The second was theme.

Wait. Neither nod nor scoff too quickly at that word. Almost everything one is taught about theme is wrong. Theme is the most malignantly balled-up notion in the whole invertebrate vocabulary of reviewing, criticism, and the teaching of how to appreciate literature and of how to write. The backup for that terrific pulpitry must wait because my topic here should not be 'Theme as an Aid to How to Read'.

It has to be narrower than that—or, at least, it must be *announced* as narrower than that—and its first presentation should be brief, almost throwaway. This is because the topic is so prickly, primitive, and prejudiced that if I tried to treat it in full right here, I'd distort the essay's apportions and probably spoil its reception in otherwise agreeable parts.

Instead, at this point I'll provide the following merciless but merciful condensation. Think of it as a brochure thrust at you on a corner, possibly advertising a forthcoming book. It would be initially addressed to those editors who have authors suffering from hyperemia, but it holds within it hints for relief of other ailments as well. These editors are looking for advice not about how to treat the written novel, but how to help the author in the *writing of* the novel. Notice how cunningly it avoids the word 'theme':

> These are things the editor should understand and be prepared to explain to the author who wants, needs, and can use them.
>
> If prelibation is an intuition of a local effect-wanted, the *master-prelibation* is the author's sense of what effect he wants the book as a whole to have,

both during the reading and when the reader comes
to the end.

The troubled writer should strive to arrive at and
fix in mind a master-prelibation, a book-spanning
effect-wanted. Often he cannot do this at the outset,
but it's essential to have it by the time the last draft
is begun.

This master-prelibation (which need not be a
'meaning', moral, statement, or subject; it can be an
observation, an insight, an emotion, an *experience*)
will guide other prelibations—ones influencing the
choice of somacluster elements, and of subsequent
events.

It's possible for the original character, circuitry,
and circumstance to be chosen in such a way that all
succeeding events are the result of character acts.
However, the author can (and usually does) cause
events (flat tires, heart attacks, the arrival of Uncle
Ben) and when he does we can give it the technical
term *accident.*

All character and author acts—all events—
should be such as to reveal or alter somacluster.
Events that don't do so should be deleted as sur-
plus.

Each event should not just *change* things; it
should advance them. The great majority of master-
prelibations entail an intensification, an accelera-
tion, aiming toward final pages that have finality.

Each element of the original somacluster, each
new event, each consequent element—and the
events *they* precipitate—should be judged by its service to the master-prelibation, its contribution to
the overriding effect-wanted. This judgment, which
should be made by sensibility and not insensate

intellect, will act as a guide to answering the most persistent and agonized query of the would-be serious novelist, which isn't "Where do I get ideas?" or "How do I get published?" It's this basic: *"How do I see what to put in and what to keep out?"*

Often the difficulty in arriving at and fixing in mind the master-prelibation is best attacked by trying to articulate it, put it into words. These words probably won't express the master-prelibation perfectly, but they can still serve the purpose of keeping the writer on course.

The key to the efficacy of the master-prelibation as a writer's guide lies in *the way it is phrased.*

The optimally phrased articulation of the master-prelibation may be called the *axiom.* The axiom, pinned to the bulletin board of the writer's mind, will serve constantly as a compass, tuning fork, stimulant, and sentinel.

The several new concepts mentioned there are amplified somewhat in the more relaxed half of this book, the Notes. In particular, you'll find there a closer look at axiom, and just what its optimal phrasing would include. I'll abandon here in the essay itself any more talk of ailments, because I'm conscious that, in emphasizing the ambulance and clinic aspect of editing, I've underplayed the joy, the thrill, the triumphant cheer that can rise with having been, however peripherally, present at the creation of a good book. Anyone who is a committed, devoted reader of fiction knows the special enjoyment that comes only from a supreme novel. But it's hard to convey the added intensity of pleasure, something close to rapture, that the editor has when the book is 'his'. He is not deluded; he knows the author has written it, not he. But still he feels a bliss of consanguinity.

My family is close to a great operatic tenor; once, I, beaming and tearful after his performance, said to him, "Why is it when *you* sing well, *I* feel proud?" And he answered, "Because you are my friend." It is that way with the editor and his author. You *do* feel pride, and privilege, and ardent comradeship, and a peculiar fulfillment as he prevails. Though I may have made it seem so, the editor's tour of duty is not confined to the medical corps. Often he is solely a gleeful witness, a willing supporter of the train, part of the swelling scene, pulled personally by the star into his celestial celebration.

Axiom, as the Notes try to show, is not 'theme', but to many writers it will smack of it, and to them theme will forever seem a naïve classroom concoction, plasticized by academics who have no idea what creative writing is really about. They can live without it, and without anyone who would press the thing on them. And the editor must grasp this: If a writer is, given his own gifts, right in rejecting any such guides, if he does not suffer from hyperemia or block or vexatious unsurety, if his narrative does move, with parts consistently contributing to an effect the writer wants, then the editor must get away from him with talk of axiom and prelibations and soma-clusters and the other office-apparatus of the diagnosing physician. Indeed the summoning forth of these lamp-tainted terms is probably always precarious and unnecessary: Any worthy diagnostic insights they enable can be conveyed in language much closer to the author's native tongue.

For the editor, the value of studying the workings of axiom and somacluster lies much less often in their influence when the editor is serving as a coach than when he is diagnosing on his own, alone. If ever he can broach them to an author who wants help with the act of writing, fine—he should have them at the ready. But their more frequent utility to him will be as tools in tracking down more or less precisely what's gone wrong in a script. The editor must, for his *own* performance, phrase the master-effect-wanted of the novel. We saw how the character grid can, after sensibility has growled unintelligibly, put its finger on what's wrong. Similarly, sensibility can complain strongly but non-explicitly when the fault is a failure of axiomatic coherence. A character can pass the test of the grid and still be irrelevant or antithetical to the master-effect the book seemingly is after. As with all internal faults, you can't assume that such strayings will be obvious to the eye. After bad sensibility, the single greatest source of inadequacy in fiction editing is the assumption that any literate reader can, without the aid of craft, naturally identify what's making the book cause the responses it evokes. If such words as *gad* and *somacluster* repel, then junk them. But don't junk the study of the forces I've used those words to denote.

More than junking the words, junk my makeshift cosmology if it doesn't strike you as right—but only if you can replace it with one of your own that you've thought through, can believe in, and can employ as a diagnostic system. My intent isn't to say these tools of mine are the ones to use, but, instead, by giving these glimpses of the complexities any determined study should uncover, to

persuade that editing simply can't be done well by winging instinct alone. Nor does 'long experience' guarantee
much. Or myrmecoid industry on the lawn of the book.
I know the dynamics of fiction are far less certain and far
more multifarious than my one-hour tour conveys. What
is certain is this: Fiction editing is hard, its subject is
complicated and its etiologies are often deep below the
surface. Therefore it demands systematic study and special training to acquire whatever insights and skills validly
apply across a wide band of orthodox narrative. We in
publishing have to recognize this and begin to do something about it. To repeat: What's needed is craft.

When I suggest the editor should be cautious about
proudly displaying to the patient his crafty scopes and
scans, I must add this: If he should be called upon to
serve as a writing coach, to tinker not with the music but
the instrument, he has to realize that even good sensibility and a fat black bag are not enough.

To succeed at such coaching requires knowledge
that is continent-wide and gold-mine-deep, not just
about his craft, but about the specific author at his door
and the infinite variety of authors in general.

He must realize what the author needs, and be stayed
by both what the author wants and what he is capable of.
There are many authors whose only scheme of writing is
to motor planlessly into midnight, looping in frustrating
circles, and up maddening dead ends—but gaining
something from each sortie until finally the ideal route
and terminus come clear. And often that's the way they
would have it be, not because they prize eyestrain, but
because they prize being at the wheel alone. They expect

and abhor artless and mediocre backseat drivers. They are among a dispersion of novelists for whom one of the great attractions of their trade is that what they do is *theirs,* worked at when, where, and how they want. No one tells them what to do. No one can yammer formula at them, or constraints of time, or an ad manager's drippy demands. The editor should understand this, and sense when his intrusion will not be justified or tolerated.

Even those writers who would prefer not to plunge alone into the dark often find that their unescorted journey is not a matter of choice, because it's only through the act of writing itself that they "find" the novel to be written.

Curiously, this intricate instinct for what an author wants and is capable of can be found in many editors. What they lack is the craft its usefulness ultimately depends on.

But this is encouraging. Craft can be taught.

I know that any text or syllabus will meet opposition, resisted by Senior Editor and by those writers for whom the whole idea is inimical. The text deserves skepticism until it proves itself, if only because, to the extent the compiler turns to editors themselves for content, he will be receiving offerings from some volunteers who are either demonstrably or secretly incompetent. Incompetence certainly has never constrained *soi-disant* writing experts from issuing *their* instructionals. This danger—of veiled incompetence in the author—comes with any textbook, however; nevertheless, we don't abandon that publishing effort.

And we shouldn't abandon it here. On my opening

page in this essay I mentioned opportunity lost and opportunity actively destroyed. The first is pitiable, the second intolerable. But both are, to some extent, meliorable, and it's that belief that has prompted this cautionary, hortative piece.

Although the argument will always be incomplete, I should now bring my part to a pause and sum it up.

The education of an editor has a prerequisite: sensibility.

His opening lesson is: First do no harm.

There is no final lesson. The learning is endless, as the learning of medicine is.

The course's syllabus would be broader than my limited citations suggest, more ramiform, and more densely foliate. Its intent would be to teach the editor the craft needed to identify the causes of reader-responses the author doesn't want, because the ultimate goal is to aid the author in achieving the effect the author is searching for.

This entails the second intent: to enable the editor to coach the author—but only if the author needs it, wants it, and can use it—in making alterations to the *written,* and even on rare occasion to the *act of writing,* aimed at finding and securing that sought-for effect.

The editor's assignment is to serve the author, because there is another diaspora of writers, comprising those isolated scribes for whom artistic seclusion is not liberty but exile, and for whom the absence of someone to talk to about their work is a loneliness beyond lovelessness. And there are others who aren't alone but are in the coils of mentors who constrict them with insensibility, ignorance, fecklessness, and malpractice. All these riven spirits deserve better, and it's for them that we should create a worldwide cadre of editors who are up to the job, a wise, sensitive, and informed guild, of which each member could be the doctor, teacher, coach, and conscience that writers and readers so vitally need.

NOTES

I have, over the years, sometimes put in the margin of a manuscript the note 'auto-comment'. It was meant to flag those passages where the author was unnecessarily or futilely excusing himself, was tediously trying to explain or biographize himself, or was repellingly congratulating himself. Still, I hate the old autocrat's dictum, "Never apologize, never explain." So I do feel that some penitence and clarifications can be useful, especially, perhaps, in a book like this, where the writer pronounces so judgmentally about other people's sensibilities. An implicit plank in his self-conferred platform is that he has a bucketful of that there sensibility stuff himself. There are various ways in which such a critic can undermine readers' confidence in his own sensibility—including by his use of humor or diction that misfires. But perhaps the most frequent mode of forfeit is the display of a seeming obtuseness about queries and complaints that his opinionated stride is causing to ripple through his audience. The infamous 'yeah-but' is not always unjustified.

This awareness means the writer, as he presents his main text, often feels faced with a dilemma: He must choose between appearing either oblivious or hobbled, his gait disjointed with pauses as he yanks on the chains of footnotes, asides, and parentheses to haul forward the ball of his self-consciousness.

My own decision has been to compromise by putting

these notes in this appendix. The essay already feels to me as cluttered as Havisham's closet, but there's still more I long to say, partly from a feeling the reader is owed it, and partly from self-indulgence. Some of what I put in these notes may excite even more skepticism or irritation than what I've already said. So I judged that, to save the central argument of the essay from being pulled under because my less essential launches fail to float, I should banish some of the more conjectural or quarrel-some stuff to the rear.

Given this, I hope you'll think of these notes as the more unguarded garrulity the speaker flops into after the lecture is over and he's sharing a beer with the hardy few that remain with him.

' H e '

I use the androgynous 'he' throughout this book. Every systematic attempt to avoid it molested the eye, ear, and mind, but I know there is no acceptable explanation or excuse to those who cannot tolerate this, so I will say only that I regret if it causes offense.

Since Jane Austen's day it's been obvious that no male novelist can surpass the effectiveness of the best women. Janet Flanner once called Katherine White "the best woman-editor in the world," a phrasing that prompts several questions: How could Flanner know? Was Flanner tacitly reserving the title 'the best editor of *all*' for a specific man she had in mind, or was her language bowed by the unenfranchised age into which she was born? I've said that the first two qualifications for editing fiction are sensibility and craft. My own experience has been this: The best reading sensibility I have ever seen closely enough for me to judge belongs to a woman, not a man. In the matter of craft, women are just as deficient as men.

N e o l o g i s m s

I'm aware that they're in here, I don't like them much myself, and I apologize for them. If I had the artistry of Freud, *as writer,* I'd be able to coin new currency that had the enduring glitter of gold. The motivation behind the effort derives from the memory of my blurred double vision as a student when I'd read a minor philosopher or critic who, instead of minting a unique new phrase for a unique new concept, would ask me to take a familiar word, rinse it of all its now-instinctive connotations, and re-stain it with an alien meaning. And sometimes he wouldn't even warn you: He'd simply escort the thing into the party unintroduced, and only after half an hour did it dawn on you, *Crikey, that's not his wife after all!* and you'd scramble back to see what blunders you'd made. Familiar-looking words inevitably are smoking thuribles trailing the incense of former meanings, associations, and confusions. In poetry this can be great; in argument it simply makes the eyes water. Thus neologisms. Sometimes a rare new strain of flower, most of the time a clanking prosthesis, obviously inanimate.

A parallel argument grants the utility and peril of arcane words. Their merits include precision, metrical or rhetorical fit, fruitful association, startling semantic epiphany. Their dangers include opacity, dislocation of attention, the uncomeliness of the unaccustomed, and the alienation of the reader who feels subjected to discourtesy and pedanticism. I personally am willing to go look a word up from time to time, but there's a part of me that says, as I heft ten pounds of Webster, "This better be worth it."

Punctuation

Punctuation shouldn't offend by profitlessly violating those schoolroom rules that literate people have come to assume, but its purpose is to tango the reader into the pauses, inflections, continuities, and connections that the *spoken* line would convey. Punctuation to the writer is like anatomy to the artist: He learns the rules so he can knowledgeably and controllédly depart from them as art requires. Punctuation is a means, and its end is: helping the reader to hear, to follow.

I d i o s y n c r a s i e s

Defying Strunk and White, I have, following a colon, started with a capital letter if what came after was a complete sentence.

I have tried to confine the use of double quotes to quotations real and imaginary, written or uttered. Single quotes are employed to indicate a *mention* of a word or term as distinguished from its *use,* and to signal that a word is suspicious, specialized, loaded with non-lexical meaning, or devolved from a quote but still trailing aromas of its former context.

I do not include within quote marks a final comma, semicolon, or period if it is not part of what I am citing.

I also may be condemned for occasionally using incomplete sentences. What nonsense. Typical of a balsa-wood ear.

I mention these things so they will not be thought inadvertencies. Far be it for me to say so, but I maintain the book has, even without them, sufficient inadvertencies to satisfy the most demanding reader.

T h e   E d i t o r ' s   L o t

Once, as a beginner, I had an experience that revealed the editor's lot to me. I was a raw and gauche assistant that you would not inflict in person on any author, but I was thought of as a good 'backroom' boy—someone at whom you could shove eleven hundred pages of chaos and demand, "Fix it!" That was my assignment on a James T. Farrell manuscript. No one had told me the difference between an editor and a rewrite man, so I toiled manically for six weeks, cutting four hundred pages, rearranging sections, rewriting sentences, rendering two hundred straight-narrative pages into scenes because the great man, then in this twilight, had simply forgotten to write dialogue. My boss did not have time to look at what I did in any detail, and the manuscript went straight into copyediting, where it fell under the eye of Frank Riley, veteran checker of scripts. I can see him now: a hundred ten pounds, very pale and gray, riven with tremors, and always seeming to smoke three cigarettes at once. "This is for you," he said, darting into my hand a memo that he had just written my boss. "In my seventeen years at Doubleday," it began, "I have never seen such a job as young McCormack has . . ." If I had had the money, I'd have hired a plane to scatter thousands of copies of the memo over New York. In fact, cross-eyed with pleasure, I promptly lost the thing.

Next came the author. Queasy with doubt, I had to bring the galleys to Farrell at his room in the Beaux Arts

Hotel. (My boss decided not to show him the postoperative manuscript; the revision was put directly into type.) Farrell sat me down and went to his desk to address his novel. He read exactly six pages. Then he turned to me. *This is it,* I felt, and I could see the headline: NOTED AUTHOR RUBS OUT SNOT-NOSED TAMPERER. What he said, in his tough-guy Chicago voice, was, "You're good, kid." Not another word about the book, and he never read more. He spent the rest of the afternoon telling me about the Black Sox scandal.

I was young and green, but after an hour's proud elation I saw the moral clear: Except for Frank Riley, no one would ever know what I'd done in my editorial servitude. In this case, not even the author. (And don't think *you* now know; underlying everything I say is this unsettling fact: For all you can be sure, I too have the sensibility of a bedpan, and I may have driven a graphite stiletto through the heart of Farrell's book. *Any* editor can summon up some self-congratulatory story.) When working at that second part of their general assignment—the editing of the script—editors are always in the 'backroom'. And I agree with Perkins: That's where we should be. I should add that my efforts did not take chaos and turn it into a great book. I never worked harder in my life, but all I managed to do was make it publishable. That too is a comment on the editor's lot.

Full Many a Gem

If it's the editor's lot to be anonymous, unobserved, unappreciated, and difficult to evaluate anyway, and if we can ask of Janet Flanner, "How could she know?" we're pressed to the further question, "How can anyone know?" In particular, what answer would I give the editor who for the last hour has been asking, "How can he impugn me this way? He doesn't know me or how I edit."

I should start by reemphasizing the distinction between sensibility and craft. I've talked to many editors about all this, and the experience has taught me to assure them early on that I'm not issuing any universal condemnation of their sensibility. Editors, understandably, reach for their guns if anyone questions their 'instinct'.

But it's not their instinct that I primarily indict. It's their craft.

Years of extended discussion with writers, agents, editors' assistants and editors themselves, and the examination of manuscripts and books and the editorial letters, memos, and marginalia behind them, and a reading through available essays and memoirs of editors past and present, have led me irresistibly to the conclusion that the whole notion of such things as a systematic editorial analysis of internal faults has been all but unheard of, unthought of.

In my conversations with editors themselves, when I *concede* instinct, brows unclench. Then when I quickly add my line about how instinct tells you *that* something

is wrong but not necessarily *what's* wrong, I have repeatedly observed a kind of churning silence fall.

There isn't a good editor alive who hasn't had moments of vexation occasioned by precisely the conjunc-
tion of total surety that a novel has gone wrong, with total
unsurety about where and why. Asked about this, not a
single editor has ever asserted to me that in fact he always
had the crafty analytic tools required to diagnose the
thing. Sometimes there is a prolonged silence, and the
moment seems almost epiphanous, as though, prior to
this instant, no inkling had ever stirred that such a craft
could and should exist.

Every line in Part Two quoting Senior Editor resist-
ing the notion of craft ("There are no rules. Everyone
knows the rules. Instinct does it all.") has been uttered
to me by experienced and often revered practitioners on
both sides of the Atlantic. Often when I did not approach
the revered personage himself, I talked to people who
worked for or with him, including novelists. I found evidence of diligence, care, and even isolated flashes of ad
hoc technique (and much expertise about the other three
aspects of an editor's job—acquiring, 'publishing', and
retaining authors). My search was long but I know it
wasn't exhaustive, so I may have missed the one we seek.
But I didn't encounter even a hint of him. In search of
Mendeleyev I found only traces of Merlin, and so I've
come to believe that there isn't a fiction editor alive who
knows as much about his craft as he ought to and could—
and this certainly includes me, despite the presumption
always implied by mounting the rostrum.

My thesis is not that at the highest levels of sensibility

the ranks are thin. Apt and exquisite responsiveness blushes unseen and unknown the whole globe round, not just in editorial realms but among the world's myriad common readers.

It's at the highest level of craft, not simply response but the constant ability to identify the cause of the response, that the ranks aren't just thin but nonexistent.

Craft, Shmaft

Let's start with a genial bit of bushwhacking by John Fowles: "I find Americans especially, the kind people who write and ask questions, have a strangely pragmatic view of what books are. Perhaps because of the miserable heresy that creative writing can be taught ('creative' is here a euphemism for 'imitative') they seem to believe that a writer always knows exactly what he's doing. . . . they believe, in short, that a book is like a machine; that if you have the knack, you can take it to bits."

The craft-crammed editor who would stride evangelistically into such a nettled camp of agnosticism would be strange indeed, and probably deserves to be ambushed. Still, I think Fowles, craftily approached, might agree that, without reducing the whole novel to a machine, one can ask valid questions about how certain aspects of the thing work.

To be fair to Fowles, we have to suspect that those American pen pals simply asked the wrong questions, or in the wrong way, because in fact his remark appears in the midst of a splendid and highly ratiocinative essay he produced about the writing of *The French Lieutenant's Woman,* in which he refers often to the "technical problems" he had to deal with. "Technical problems" inevitably suggests questions of craft. So I maintain that Fowles, irked by colonial naïfs, strayed into an inconsistency he would not cling to.

I continue to uphold a sharp distinction between the craft of editing the novel and the craft of writing it (and

I'd also maintain that the phrase 'the craft of the novel' is a solecism because 'craft' entails activity; a novel may be a result of craft but it's not itself an agent; however, that way lies linguistic pettifoggery beyond even what I can accept here). The point is that some writers, like most editors, both abjure and respect craft. Why?

Norman Mailer helps us: "I'm a bit cynical about craft. I think there's a natural mystique in the novel which is more important than craft. . . . I think of craft as being a St. Bernard dog with that little bottle of brandy under his neck. Whenever you get into *real* trouble the thing that can save you as a novelist is to have enough craft to be able to keep warm long enough to be rescued. Of course this is exactly what keeps good novelists from becoming great novelists. Robert Penn Warren might have written a major novel if he hadn't had just that little extra bit of craft to get him out of all the trouble in *All the King's Men*. . . . I think . . . the adoration of craft . . . is fatal for somebody who has a large ambition and a chance of becoming a great writer."

This is Mailer talking a generation ago, when, one feels, he often overstated things in order to burst himself through to insights that would never surrender themselves to cooler reflectiveness. And we do garner what he's after here. The writer who, heaving on the ocean of art, timidly clings to the raft of craft will never plunge to those unfathomed caves. But focus on Mailer's line about craft's being able to keep you warm long enough to be rescued. By what? By the natural "mystique" of prelibations that are not simply mechanical products of craft. And by imagination. And sensibility. Which is, evidently, what got him into a fix in the first place. So I'd adjust his image. It's *craft* that does the *rescuing.* The pearl-diver, heaved and disoriented, gropes desperately up to the raft where he can catch his breath and bearings. There are many writers, like Auden, for whom that raft had not just a ladder, but a diving board.

It will be argued that craft doesn't tell an *editor* how to do his job either, because all the decisions are made by sensibility. There's truth in this, but the essential point to notice is that, though it's sensibility that does the weighing, diagnosis is needed to hunt down what goes on the scale.

Sensibility—with the aid of intelligence and memory—commissions craft, designs it. Which is to say that sensibility notices how, often, an undesirable effect it detects is traceable to a generic fault in the narrative. This means that new craft will arise for so long as sensibility continues to notice failings that are generically new, or that heretofore have been so internally obscured to us that they have defied anatomizing and codification.

Craft, to the writers and editors who know that art and instinct are the essential things, looks like an upstart, a parvenu of our analytic age, a stagehand who has taken to asking, "How did you like my performance tonight?"

I gladly concede this point outright. Every great performer in every art was taught some craft at some time. But that did not make him what he is. Others were taught the same, yet they're not artists. Always: Craft does not do it; it only allows it to get done.

Accident

All events in a novel are either character-acts or author-acts—that is, accidents. All changes in circumstance and circuitry are caused by a character—or the author—doing something.

Of course we know it's the author who causes the character to act, and to act the way he does. But most writers would agree with the distinction between acts predicated by the character's internal makeup and those events the writer makes happen. Writers frequently talk about characters 'taking over', running out of control, not doing what the writer wants them to do. Or sometimes doing things the writer never expected. This isn't to say that the author's prelibation is no longer obtaining. It is. It's listening to what has gone before, to what was still to come (which may now be fading like a station on our car radio as we drive deeper into the country), and to that beckoning master-prelibation, the more (or less) sharply foreseen total-effect-wanted of the book. But though prelibation's current "And now *this!*" originates in the author's own plasma, it's often in response to the roiling of creatures of imagination so intensely and fully filled-in they wrench free of their creator, attaining the 'otherness' that so astonishes parents in their children.

Authors have even reported characters running so amok as to abort the book, meaning that their actions made impossible the fulfillment of the master-prelibation they had in mind. (Auchincloss: " . . . the first version of [*The Rector of Justin*], in which [Griscam] appeared, had to be scrapped entirely when his personality got out of hand.") Forced to choose between their plans and the insurgent devil-child, they suppress the palace revolution by killing the rebel. Other authors have reported *going with* the compelling spirit, almost rejoicing in the possession, in becoming an amanuensis to imagination.

The writer who prefers to continue to pursue his original effect-wanted has, we can say, made an error in setting up his somacluster. If we agree that each element should contribute to effecting the master-prelibation, then we might say of a given script, where we know the author's hopes, that he miscalculated circuitry: These characters don't ally, clash, complement, and orchestrate in a way that has the effect wanted.

So that's what we mean by 'accident': author-acts as distinguished from character-acts.

Purists will call for accident to be kept to a minimum. But in fact some of the keenest and most seizing moments we've all experienced in good books have come from accident the author has dreamed up. Accident often provides the moment in the novel when the shriek of life becomes most audible.

Purists aren't all insensitive to this. They're against *bad* accident. It's accepted that, up to a point, accident that puts characters *into* a testing situation is okay; it's when it gets them *out* of it that we complain.

So accident *can* be a nuisance, but, to vary Mailer's point, so can the novel that is too 'well made', too controlled. The editor's job is emphatically not to impose neatness on the novel. A novel I edited last year was seen in early draft by an outside reader who declared that it

should be polished, 'cleaned up', the streaming liquefac-
tion of its clothes bound tidily away. But I knew that the
jagged, throeful intensity was exactly what made the
book special, and to take it out would be to lobotomize
it. The book was edited, but in other ways intended to
enhance its effect on its ideal intended audience. She, the
cool outsider, was not and never would be a member of
that audience, and thus both author and editor would
have been wrong to try to recut the key to fit her lock.

Even Euclid admits of curves. The writer who too
controlledly indites his linear doings can leave us chilled.
But don't assume that craft necessarily leads to this. Indeed, the best of diagnostic craft, summoned by sensibility, will detect when minimalism has become anorexia.

The original circumstance, and the circuitry, and the
very character of the characters are all, in effect, accidents the author has decreed. The characters, with their
in-built powers and inclinations, will dodge and hammer
each other and their circumstance, and they will change
the shape of the somacluster as the book goes on. But the
author is constantly making changes too, expanding and
altering circuitry, and circumstance, looking always for
new gads.

Situation is seldom an immovable monolith, given at
the outset, upon which the character and author can
merely doodle a forlorn graffiti. Motion in narrative is the
sum of all character- and author-acts. Every one of these
acts should serve to reveal or alter elements of character
or situation. Ideally, the editor has the superb sensibility
required to realize that, say, Melville's 'Whiteness' chapter is not a superfluous interpolation but a profoundly

effective piece of *setting,* as we would grant of "It was the best of times, it was the worst of times. . . ."

The question ultimately to be addressed is: What should go in it? That is, what initial somacluster and then what acts to reveal it and change it?

The flood, air raid, heart attack, cancer are author-imposed accidents, but so are the small haps of life. Chris is in the elevator; she is late and she is anxious. Just as the door is about to close, Andy arrives (accident). He doesn't see Chris; he belts the closing door. The elevator gets stuck (accident). Andy at last gets it going and they reach the street, only to find that during the delay Chris's car has been towed away (accident). Ah, but Andy has a car (accident). And so on through the jig of haps that screenwriters are so adept at inventing.

It's useless to maintain that these small-hap accidents are all directly entailed by the master-prelibation. Imagination, often just a contractor working on orders from the architect-staff of prelibation, obviously is not restricted to the large strategic questions of a city planner. It also must cope with immediate tactical problems: Forget the grand avenue scheme for a moment; how do I get these bricks of narrative up to the third floor?

The author has to build the structure in the first place, using certain accidents like a ladder—necessary, but not part of the edifice itself. Then he usually wants to see the structure changed—by him, to provide new gads, or by characters who make things happen. If all of the essential changes are by act of author rather than character, the book probably feels silly.

Even the one-character novel—Juan crashes in the

jungle alone and has to walk out—hasn't just one circumstance. Within circumstance, the jungle is the setting. But the gads change: Now it's killer ants, now lack of water, now a surging river to cross. You may not want to write about Indiana Jones; you may prefer Candide or Augie March; but whomever you choose, you have to realize that characters are satisfyingly portrayed only through gadded action. If the characters are not gadding one another, then the author must do it—by an accidental event that alters the situation. An intentional accident. What controls accident is prelibation. What influences those ground-level prelibations is the master-prelibation hovering moonlike in the sky of the book. I say 'influences' rather than 'controls' because, as we've noted, prelibations are not always fully under rein; they can go berserk, mutiny, or just lose their way.

What we're working toward is an idea of how to increase the strength of master-prelibation's influence, its tidal pull, if we have reason to believe that, on a given book, such greater control would be a good thing. But to reach that peak in Darien, we need first to climb a few other notional hills.

I n i t i a

To most of us who are addictedly absorbed by the process of writing, initia are intrinsically engaging. But there are even a couple of practical values to perusing them.

What's an initium? Broadly, it's what the author had in mind when he began his novel. We can ask, "What do you mean by 'had in mind'?" or "When does a writer actually 'begin' his novel?" or any number of similar questions, but I think the best way into this is by example. Here's a list of the sorts of things writers report as what I've call 'initia':

"A vision of what this street looked like in 1906."

"A pretty girl with a limp, that I once saw on the ferry."

"My mother."

"Queen Elizabeth the First."

"The Mafia."

"Turn-of-the-century America."

"What would have happened if John F. Kennedy had not died [if the South had won the Civil War . . . if the Nazis had won . . . if there were a nuclear holocaust]?"

"What if a Rockefeller daughter fell in love with a Communist [a President's daughter with a terrorist . . . a bigot's daughter with a black . . . a cardinal with a nun . . . a feminist with a chauvinist . . . Caesar with Cleopatra]?"

"A news story I read about a young man who drowned his pregnant girlfriend."

"Keeping the reader guessing, and constantly surprising him, about whodunit." (Yes, just this much is enough to sit a mystery writer at his desk; it is the dominant element of his master-prelibation—the *feeling* he wants. Other writers might exclaim that this doesn't supply a thing—no character, no circumstance, no key event—but as we'll see when we examine what, say, Doctorow and Didion begin with, the mystery writer, given just this feeling-wanted, has a fine head start.)

"Gripping the reader with the characters' struggle to get off the icecap [save the farm . . . win the bicycle race . . . rob the museum]." (Here the writer has both the feeling and a circumstance.)

"What would happen if Goldie Hawn joined the army [a crime-fighting D.A. were sent to a penitentiary filled with killers he'd convicted . . . a man invented a synthetic fiber that felt as good as cotton or wool, never wore out, and never needed cleaning or pressing . . . a doctor in a spa-community discovered that the waters were polluted]?"

"Keeping the reader gripped with terror from fear of the Aliens."

"Sexual obsession."

"The experience of the jungle war and how men reacted differently to it."

"The nature and effect of the rat race in . . . [law, advertising, Hollywood, politics]."

"The way power corrupts . . . [in politics, business, occupying armies]."

"The way religiosity produces hypocrisy and stunted lives."

"Conveying the anguish and despair of a woman who has lost her religion."

"The way a certain marriage went from bliss to agony to dissolution."

"The way a certain kind of strong person can be brought down by his sense of responsibility for a 'weaker' dependent."

"The way some women write, produce, and direct their own victimization."

"The way a brave and good man, in a selfish, prejudiced community, can . . . [triumph, be ruined]."

Those are all initia, but you'll notice they range from the merest tickle in the mind to fully articulated ideas of the form college teachers would accept as 'themes'. My subject is 'theme as a writer's tool'. So, first, I ask you to forget schoolroom fiats that 'themes' can only be in the form of a moral, generalized statement, 'meaning', or some other single stipulated genus. That's wrong. For the writer's purpose a 'theme' can be subject, topic, mood, emotion, observation, experience, 'plot', 'story', or 'other'.

Having made my formal bow to this school-wrecked term (Conrad: "old, old words, worn thin, defaced by ages of careless usage"), I'll hereafter avoid 'theme' as much as possible. For that concept adjusted in ways I'll soon try to explain, I'll use the word *axiom*. (Yes, it's unlovable, almost forbidding; but the dozen alternative terms I weighed were each susurrous with still other connotations I did not want.) In the essay I said that the master-prelibation is the intuition of the master-effect the author wants his book as a whole to have. The articulation of that effect-wanted is the axiom. The key to the usefulness of the axiom as a guide is the way it is phrased. [See the next Note, *Axiom Axiom.*]

The axiom, crouched constantly in the prompter's pit of the mind, is what should serve as that compass, tuning fork, stimulant, and sentinel as he addresses the question of "what to put in it". The axiom should guide the sub-prelibations, the page-to-page intuitions that instruct and direct imagination as it conjures up the narrative.

Sometimes the effect-wanted *is* a statement or moral, or, more correctly, the *acceptance* of a statement or moral. We'll get back to all this, but first let's roughly break that list of initia into four groups. Remember, an initium is only what sparked the writer in the first place. Often it's a long way from yet yielding a master-prelibation.

In the first group, the writer has no idea what effect he'll eventually want to aim at—no pole star of mood, subject, message, emotion, anything, except a teasing sperm still looking for its egg.

In the second, he has a subject, but often the master-prelibation is still inchoate. He feels there's something effective to be done with the material, but he's not yet sure what it will be.

In the third, he's content not even to probe for a master-effect. He simply wants to start with a 'what if'—a volatile state of affairs he's sure will produce specific gads. He almost prefers the uncertainty that will make him nearly as much a spectator of the evolving narrative as the reader is.

In the fourth, the author is clear about at least one effect he wants to achieve—a grip he wants to enforce, a vision he wants to convey, a particular story he wants to tell.

In Part Three I said it's essential that the editor be aware of and appreciate the infinite variety of writers at their work. I stress this again here, as I broach the idea of an 'axiom', because whenever I exhort such things as systems and grids I get goosebumps myself as I sense the hackles rise out there, particularly on writers. I say again: The techniques I have been urging in the approach to, and execution of, the job, is for *editors.* It's not meant to tell writers how to do it. Most writers do concede their need for craft, and it's pretty to think *some* of these tools will be helpful to *some* of them—including the concept of axiom. But it's important that editors realize there are many writers who will bolt away from such ratiocinative stuff.

It's not that these writers fear thinking about what they're doing. But most of them feel they must think about it in their own way. The editor who doesn't bother to discern what his author's way *is* is likely at last to get thrown out on his however exquisite ear.

To pursue this lesson for editors, let's go back to the first group of initia. Is it possible that anybody starts a novel with no idea of what's going to be in it? Here's the testimony of a writer who is himself a former editor and teacher:

E. L. Doctorow: "With the beginnings of the work, you really don't know what's going to happen. . . . It's not calculated at all. . . . One of the things I had to learn as a writer was to trust the act of writing. To put myself in the position of writing to find out what I was writing."

The first initium above—the street in 1906—was Docto-row's, the day he began *Ragtime*. He reports he had no idea where that street would lead.

Doctorow is not alone. Joan Didion: "The whole question of how you work out your narrative is very mysterious. It's a good deal more arbitrary than most people who don't do it would ever believe. . . . At the beginning I don't have anything at all, don't have any people, any weather, any story. . . ." The interviewer then gave Didion the remark that Doctorow would echo years later: "So the process of writing the novel is for you the process of discovering the precise novel you want to write?" "Exactly."

Think of this "finding", this discovering, as the process of arriving at the master-prelibation, which will then guide the writer in such things as selecting his people. But I know there is delicacy of judgment needed here, like that of, not just when, but if ever to make a pass at the object of your affections. If I had to guess, I'd say that, for Didion, the prospect of an early planning session with an editor to talk about optimal somacluster would have all the appeal of a self-help lab in bestiality.

The greatest fear about editors is that they will be "meddlesome"—mostly with the music, but also with the instrument producing it. Even though one of my theses is that editors don't contribute *enough,* I agree with the fear, and I don't think this is an inconsistency since my more correctly stated gripe is that editors don't contribute enough that's *good.* "Meddlesome" work by an editor is malpractice that issues from his bad sensibility, inadequate craft, and leaden splashings into art—shortcomings that are endemic in publishing.

Conceding all that, I nevertheless yet again shuffle back to the position that a *good* editor could benefit, at some time or other, any writer who ever lived.

Doctorow has an image that he uses to explain a novelist's setting off in the dark: "It's like driving a car at night. You never see further than your headlights, but you can make the whole trip that way." The image is fetching to look at, but frail when handled. As you drive, headlights will keep you from interrupting a tree, but when you reach a fork in the road, their destinationless beam will not tell you where you want to go or which road will get you there.

A pleasant Sunday's drive can have exactly that aimless self-referential quality, but Doctorow is not a practitioner of meta-fiction. His point, of course, is that when he starts out he doesn't know where he wants to go. But then he adds two pertinent remarks: "I don't think anything I've written has been done in under six or eight drafts," and, "At a certain point you figure out what your premises are and what you're doing."

What do you suppose he has in mind with that last sentence?

In the essay I said there are indeed writers for whom the only way to find the itinerary is by motoring planlessly into midnight.

The writing hand does *discover,* unlidding implications of character, circuitry, and circumstance that were not thought of as the batch was mixed in the lab. Or, like an inventor tinkering with parts until he suddenly divines what his new invention might be, he realizes some parts currently on the workbench don't fit in even as ornaments, while other, missing, parts must now be found.

Still, I want to believe that if writers like Doctorow had an informed confidant with whom they could, *when they wanted to,* craftily consider such things as 'premises' and 'what you're doing', they *might* reach their destinations in less than six or eight drafts. But I concede: only *might.* Moreover (and this observation is not occasioned by any faults in a Doctorow novel), even eight drafts are no guarantee that a novelist has ever got his master-prelibation clear, and thus his choice of somacluster elements, and of accident, may be unsure.

Few serious writers feel in retrospect that all their books display the same optimal level of achievement. Why not? Because, in some instances at least, something was basically awry—something in the somacluster perhaps, the character circuitry, the situation design, or (and some writers have said as much) what I've called the 'axiom'. Something that, all through the writing, was hampering performance like an undetected abscess. Something that, in theory, a good editor might have spotted early on.

But we were talking about initia and axioms.

John Gardner used to instruct his students: "Start with character." But Gardner was himself a novelist, and most—not all—novelists have a tendency to believe that the way they do it is the only way it can be done. (Another one of Gardner's allegedly basic instructions for developing a narrative was: "Get in a trance.") Under Gardner, Doctorow would not have started *Ragtime.* A reasonable modification of Gardner's line would seem to be: "Don't start *without* character," and an editor who was an insensible mechanic of somacluster might urge this 'rule' on his author.

But we've seen that a rule like this is absurd for two reasons.

First, the unignorable fact is that powerful initia arise where there's no character yet firmly in sight.

Second, good writers have given testimony that we can interpret as implying that they can't possibly work out the characters until they have, say, clarified what the situation is. Or even what master-effect they're after.

Still, it's also an unignorable truth that very many writers always do start with character.

All of which gives us the clue to another potential usefulness in examining initia (beyond the one of educating editors about the varieties of creative style they must be prepared for). If the editor knows what the initium was, it can alert him to look for typic weaknesses that tend to accompany typic initial strengths.

Different initia bring with them different perils. Part of Kerr's point in complaining about the wooden quality of problem plays was that the followers of Ibsen were long on circumstance and short on character. Which yields the first hint for the editor: If the author is telling him about a new novel he is planning, and he reveals that the initium was a 'lesson', the editor should be on guard against shallow characters. If the initium was a character, beware of gadless circumstance. Look too for unsloped circumstance if the initium was a circuitry. A hurly-burly of angry young folk can be colorful and incandescent but ultimately unsatisfying because, though the circuitry may glow red, and in the end the figures are rearranged on the stage, our gut feels deprived somehow. There have been successful dramas and novels of self-revelation, of talk, but those that fail despite their crystal or neon writing do so usually because the writer has not created a sloped circumstance: an occasion for a change of situation between beginning and end, a change that is more than that of the character's 'understanding', a change that is brought about by character *acts*. For our purposes an act need not be confined to something that comes out of a gun; it *can* be an utterance but only if the utterance *affects someone other than the utterer*. This isn't to say that all self-revelation should be deleted, but rather that if the novel is *only* that, the reader will, however liminally, feel underfed.

Self-revelation that *leads to action* within the drama is an improvement. Say the circumstance is that the top job is open and four people show up in the boss's parlor to interview for it. Much sphincter-rending colloquy follows. They all end up naked and exposed. Can be vibrant stuff. But it probably won't be adequate if the *circumstance* as described is no different at the end from the beginning. We need, say, one character to 'discover' he doesn't really want the job, and another to see that he isn't up to it, so they quit the competition. But even then I'll bet we'd be longing for resultive *inter*action among some of the players.

If the initium is a *topic* or subject, the editor should help the author eventually to focus on the need to bring in an *attitude* or *emotion*. We have all seen exquisitely phrased and exact presentations of characters who nevertheless don't interest us; we just don't care about them one way or another.

If the initium is a setting, look for unsloped circumstance, bereft of true issues. The author dwells on the colorful and detailed trappings of the Prince of Wales's entourage in 1935, and the cluttered story cranks to a halt for lack of actual gads. A few obviously papier-mâché tigers are groaned halfheartedly into place, but what the author is really about is Vienna! Shanghai! Gstaad! You should have seen them when! But a travelogue is not a novel.

When the initium is an exotic predicament there are special dangers. (Prototypically an airplane is involved: It crashes in the Kalahari, on an icecap, to the ocean floor, into outer space—or it's hijacked.) Long experience teaches editors that the first usual failing to be on guard against is the author's total absorption with the hardware and the hard science. So, preoccupied with setting and nonhuman gads, he neglects his people. The second failing sounds like the opposite but isn't: He goes mad for circuitry. But his circuit is fabricated of parts as inorganic and standard as the plane itself. "Let's have a hero and a coward, a humanitarian and a greedy capitalist, a heroine and a chauvinist, a black and a bigot!" Unfortunately the mind that thinks this way after the age of twenty-five will probably be a hack forever. All the editor can do is control the damage and live with the awful devilishness of the God of Gifts—the fiendish deity who so often makes the hack a genius at gads and accident, and the fine, persuasive portrait artist a story idiot.

The third danger of the novel started from an all-in-a-fix-together premise is that it will turn into an endless series of flashbacks. Three-dimensioned characterization through plausible, consequential, current action is an ideal beyond many writers; either they give no history and rely on performances as broad as in a silent movie; or, with one momentum-slugging flashback after another, these ancient scriveners yank us off to kitchens long ago and far away so we can see how all the characters got to be the way they are.

Of course the editor doesn't have to know the initium in order to register these flaws for what they are. But should the author call him in at the planning stage, it's useful if the editor has the experience—or the textbook of craft—to make him aware of the potential curse that comes with certain kinds of initia. He can help the author to see the danger in setting out from home having thought through only one of the elements that will be necessary for a successful journey.

The writer who commences his novel with a what-if initium is in an exciting but unsure position. He knows his interest—seeing what's going to happen—but he doesn't know the effect he wants. He wants it to be 'gripping', but 'grip' is not a feeling, it's the result of a feeling. Since he doesn't know how it's going to end up, what's going to happen, he's not sure of the action, mood, emotion, insight, he'll at last want to have effected.

He has the advantage of starting out with one aspect of mood: tension. And it could all sustain and work out wondrously, but it's a gamble. Fully as many abortive missions start with 'what if' initia as with the merest gamete. With both, the author has the assignment of, at some time during the writing, reaching the point where his prelibations are channeled not just by the artless Brownian movement of the fixed ingredients, but by a master-effect-wanted. He may have intuited his dancers, but he has left the choreography and even the kind of music to them.

The dangers of a what-if initium with minimal given elements are those described above as coming with an initium that's solely character, solely circumstance, solely circuitry—no motion, no substance, no development.

The 'let's see' attitude is enticing to certain minds, like skydiving. I don't scorn daring, but still I want to see craft in packing the parachute and picking a landing area. I recall one famous writer of a generation ago who was resolutely against planning anything. "If I knew what was going to happen I'd be too bored to write it." His career was marked, after early success, by constant failure.

The fourth class of initia—the ones beginning "the way that power corrupts in politics," etc.—are uttered by writers who are, on average, the most likely to formalize their axiom and forge through. True, they are ultimately at the mercy of their imagination and sensibility, but they won't find prelibation forsaking them. Higher-level prelibations, anyway. Implied ones. At the lawn-level of individual words and phrases, where Dickens's 'unnecessary details' teem, a brilliant axiom may still be a dim light. But it can expose a mood-wrong joke. It can note that the fact that he takes cream in his coffee does not characterize the strongman, though it may his brother who always laments his weight.

However, it's in this fourth class that the 'message' initia lie, so watch for characters that are either wooden or skeletal.

Setting should not sprawl garrulously, but it must be vivid and convincing. Characters must have those few 'unnecessary' shadings that give them a believable life offstage. The cast must not be so lean as to feel unlifelike, as when the playwright is squeezed by a producer thinking of salary costs.

Often the writer who commences his book with a well-developed initium has in fact gone far beyond initium already: He knows what's going to happen in the novel. And, lest in citing Doctorow and Didion I suggest theirs *is* the only way it get done, I should quote E. M. Forster: "The novelist should, I think, always settle when he starts what is going to happen, what his major event is to be. He may alter this event as he approaches it, indeed he probably will, indeed he probably had better, or the novel becomes tied up and tight. But the sense of a solid mass ahead, a mountain round or over or through which the story must somehow go, is most valuable and, for the novels I've tried to write, essential."

But then Forster, with the teasing inconsistency you learn to expect when writers talk about writing, adds: "When I began *A Passage to India* I knew that something important happened in the Malabar Caves, and that it would have a central place in the novel—but I didn't know what it would be."

Still, writers other than Forster corroborate his essential point. For example, they will report that the initial beacon for the whole book was a certain climactic scene, a scene they can describe vivaciously in terms of tone and effect ("Everyone realizes—or is made to face—how inadequate and self-deluding they've been.") without any firm idea of what specific characters or concrete issues will fill out the scene.

That good critic Malcolm Cowley, on reading Forster's remarks, said: "Most novelists . . . are like the chiefs of an exploring expedition. They know who their companions are (and keep learning more about them); they know what sort of territory they will have to traverse on the following day or week; they know the general object of the expedition, the mountain they are trying to reach, the river of which they are trying to discover the source. But they don't know exactly what their route will be, or what adventures they will meet along the way, or how their companions will act when pushed to the limit."

John Irving could not be farther from Doctorow: "I knew everything that was going to happen, in advance. . . . *I want to know how a book feels after the main events are over.* [My italics—TM.] The authority of the storyteller's voice—of mine, anyway—comes from knowing how it all comes out before you begin. . . . I have last chapters in my mind before I see first chapters. . . . I love plot, and how can you plot a novel if you don't know the ending first? How do you know how to introduce a character if you don't know how he ends up? You might say I back into a novel. All the important discoveries—at the end of a book—these are the things I have to know before I know where to begin."

A skeptic might say, well, that just shows that Irving sketches the novel out in his head before he puts line one on paper. So really his writing of the novel doesn't begin with line one; it begins the day he starts thinking about it. So we have no idea what his initia are like, how he discovers master-prelibation. Doctorow's first five drafts are *his* thinking about it.

But Bernard Malamud was like Irving: "When I start I have a pretty well developed idea of what the book is about and how it ought to go, because generally I've been thinking about it and making notes for months, if not years. Generally I have the ending in mind, usually the last paragraph almost verbatim. I begin at the beginning and stay close to the track, if it is a track and not a whalepath. If it turns out I'm in the open sea, my compass is my narrative instinct, with an assist by that astrolabe, theme. The destination is . . . already defined." For 'compass' read 'prelibation'; for 'astrolabe' read 'masterprelibation'.

In the cases of the DA in jail and Goldie Hawn in the army, the initium has the advantage of consisting of two elements: character and circumstance. But something of the same generic liability looms: The author will thoroughly think out solely one character, and the trappings of circumstance. The editor should promote consideration of circuitry and sufficient characterization of the others in that circuit.

In the end, all these considerations begin to suggest that the first step toward an artful framing of an axiom will be to bring initia together, create a family that can procreate. Subject needs emotion. They both need circuitry, which needs circumstance. Mood needs action. Sermon needs character.

An ideally phrased axiom, arrived at early in the writing, is the best preventive of writer's block, hyperemia, bulimia, and anorexia. And so to the next Note, in which we see how a writer might climb from initium to masterprelibation, and the editor might record the moment in an axiom.

Axiom   Axiom

The premise in this Note is that the *phrasing* of the axiom will be crucial to its efficacy as a guiding tool for the editor (and the writer who uses one.)

A reminder: The *axiom* is the *verbal expression* of the *master-prelibation,* the statement of the effect-wanted of the book as a whole.

But wait: Why does the editor need this kind of 'guiding tool'? What does he use it for?

The editor should work out an axiom for books of any complexity because, among other reasons, he's going to need all the help he can get in the diagnosing of a common ailment: the parasitic lodging in the manuscript of something that is irrelevant or even antithetical to the author's master-prelibation. If you don't have some kind of articulate grasp of what the author is trying to do to the reader's intellect and emotions, you are liable to flounder, to overlook the very thing you should spot, as you are whenever you've been given a foggy, non-explicit work assignment.

The editor also needs this verbal expression of the effect-sought because chances are he's going to have to *talk* about it as he tries to convey his points to the author—and words are among the handiest things we have to talk with

A character can sometimes pass the test of the character grid (and a scene may even get through a scene grid) and still not belong in the book. (Fitzgerald used to read portions of *Tender* aloud to friends. Edmund Wilson reports that after such a reading to Dos Passos that included a particularly brilliant passage, FSF asked JDP how he liked it. JDP said he did like it, "all except that part that's so wonderful." FSF asked what he meant. JDP said, "Oh, you know: That part that's so perfectly marvelous." Wilson claims that FSF cut the passage; it's not to be found in the final *Tender.*)

For the Luddites, an assurance: I mean to advance the axiom as an *editorial* tool. I'm aware that many writers will either shrink from it or simply find it unusable. Not all writers. Henry James was not the only novelist to keep extensive notebooks in which he talked himself forward from 'germ', to subject, to the poignant or piquant effect-wanted. Such entries amount to accounts of how the master-prelibation was arrived at. Its final articulation is what, in its most utile form, I'm calling 'axiom'. If the remarks in this Note about what the optimal axiom should contain—about the kinds of things that should be encompassed in the most decisive, indicative, governing, auspicious master-prelibations—are of use to some authors, I'll be pleased. But I have no illusions that they could or should be heeded by all writers.

I'm also aware that many great works are not readily captured with this editorial butterfly net. Go dash off 'the' axiom for Hamlet. Maybe He could do it, but I won't try. (Few of us have ever seen that entire play performed; it can take over five hours, and modern directors regularly excise whole sections. These directors, presumably, *do* have, as *all* directors presumably do, an axiom in mind, an announceable effect that all their shapings are bent on achieving.)

Though I assume all successful works of art are more

or less guided by a master-prelibation, I concede it usually remains implicit, inverbal. I've already asserted that we don't 'think' in words. A corollary to that assertion may be that there are 'thoughts' that can *never* be put into words. In some sense, *no* thoughts or feelings can be 'put into' words. All we can hope for is to come up with verbal expressions such that, when they are heard or read, they will cause the reader to 'have in mind' what the writer had as he wrote them. The philosopher may say, "Whereof one cannot speak, thereof one must be silent," but precisely the challenge in talking about art is in finding the border of that 'whereof'. Some aspects of prelibation may be beyond articulation, but some seem not to be. The writer, and his editor, should always believe that at least some part of 'what I'm trying to do here' can be spoken of. The axiom is meant to be a tool, a reminder, a guide. So think of it pragmatically: If you can phrase something that, pinned to the bulletin board of your mind, *works,* however imperfectly, use it. Forget perfection. We'll never reach it. But there are worthy achievements available this side of it.

If it is not optimally phrased, an axiom can be misdirected, incomplete, too loose, too static. Here is an outline of at least some of the functions an optimally phrased axiom should serve.

Above all, it must stress the effect-wanted. This is not an impressionist fiat saying the focus must always be on textless sensation, mood music, laving tides of emotion. A novelist can certainly be motivated by the desire to convey a lesson or an insight. But in axiom form his aim should be phrased as an embracing *acceptance* of the lesson and *understanding* of the insight. The axiom that the editor (or author) draws up must always be in terms of a *result* in the reader's head, heart, gut. This means that, almost always, master-prelibations of lesson or insight must be fortified with emotion. The emotion serves as the binder, the fixative. Without this emotive supplement, lessons and insights may be clear but unembraced. In other words the total master-effect-wanted will not be achieved.

There are master-prelibations in which the effect sought is directly an experience, emotion, or story. As we'll see, thus-motivated authors often actively profess no interest in moral, homily, generalization.

Second, the axiom should function to *exclude*, to focus, to screen out the irrelevant and anti-axiomatic.

Don't worry that this excluding function necessarily means a skeletal book. The focused mind will see *more* that's pertinent. There is greater vivid detail in one plane of sharp focus than in an infinite depth of field that is soft-focus throughout. Think of the plane as being determined by the master-prelibation. One of the pillars supporting master-prelibation is the author's awareness of the peculiar satisfaction, a basic component in aesthetic pleasure, that the reader gets from sensing that everything in the novel fits, applies, locks into, and stems out of everything else. It might be interesting to consider why this is so, because the reasons just might help us to fine-tune the concept of 'axiom', but I know I won't manage that here. Think of exclusion as having the merits of weeding and pruning in the garden; or think of it as refining and reducing the area of impact, and thus increasing and enhancing the accuracy, control, penetration, and pleasure.

Moreover, consider the result of inadequate exclusion. "I want to talk about the plight of man today!" What aspect? "Every aspect!" It won't work. The impulse has no practical guiding value because it has no excluding power.

(Now, looking back at the famous spar between Wolfe and Fitzgerald in which Wolfe celebrated himself and Sterne as great putter-inners content to let Fitzgerald and Flaubert flea-pinch their lives away as taker-outers, we think of Wolfe's apparent moot-court win as a fiasco of eloquence. Wolfe and Sterne have joined the other woolly mammoths, while Fitzgerald and Flaubert flourish nimbly.)

A writer with initial block may claim that excluding axioms are the last thing he needs. Maybe he's right. But I'm not convinced that holds in all cases. How many of us have seen someone who is free to choose his own assignment, but who freezes at his desk because, by constantly gazing at the whole vast chart of possibility, he never gets close enough to any segment to pick out a path of access. He's like a mountain climber who never gets started because from ten miles away he can't perceive any handholds. In publishing, the prudent editorial director who has a thus-immobilized but talented acquiring editor will think to restrict his area of attention. "Jim, we need some sports books," or "What about Hollywood? How about some female star over fifty who hasn't told her story?" Specificity of assignment is often the precise enabler needed. It's important to realize that one of the implications of the wide variety in writers is that there are many who need and want guidance.

The third function of the axiom should be to move

the focus toward *activity.* Not 'the Panama Canal' but 'the building of the Panama Canal'. Not 'my mother' but 'the way my mother ruined our lives by . . .' These aren't complete axioms yet, but they're closer than a static noun.

Before moving on to examine some specific axioms, I should yet again remind editors: Don't ever try to mandate or even expect a writer to specify an axiom before he starts his book, or, for that matter, *ever* to specify it. We do have accounts of authors who, on a literal bulletin board above their desks, have posted general mottoes and even specific directives for a given book. If they find the framing of an axiom a congenial thing, fine. You, the editor, should work toward one for your own purposes. Surprisingly, you may find authors willing to help *you* in your diligent, interesting labor. Can't hurt, that. The writer should, before his last draft is begun, have a master-prelibation in mind. The editor, wanting to frame an axiom for his own work, can sometimes serve that purpose, *and* the objective of enhancing the master-prelibation in the author's mind, by mulling the whole thing over out loud with the writer.

An editor is talking with his author. He is asking her: What *about* your mother? You don't mean a photographic portrait, a still-shot giving every detail—her favorite colors, the recipe for homemade peach ice cream, her seventh-grade teacher's name? "No," says the author. "She was so smart, and so pretty—and so unhappy. And she made people around her unhappy." Just through her appearance? "No, by what she *did."*

Good, we're excluding, and we're moving toward activity. To what *end* can't be far behind.

The author begins to understand that to make the reader see and feel what she wants, an exhaustive inventory of facts would be irrelevant.

Don't list all Mother's lecture dates between 1958 and 1963. But do examine her role in the circuitry of her family and friends. Do select those friends for their gad value—which means how they caused changes in her feeling or actions, or how they prompted her to characteristic behavior. And pick people who will show what effect Mother could have. Given the necessities for vivid and convincing setting, confine all other displays of circumstance to those that will gad Mother to those responses that will reveal essential aspects of her character or that will change her circuitry or circumstance. Any scene that leaves circuitry and circumstance as it was before, or that redundantly displays an essential facet of character that has already been optimally conveyed, or that conveys another facet (her loathing for Japanese food) that is never itself manifested or echoed in any other core-characteristic responses or action—these (like 'Joe Harkness', the false-lead bartender's name) should all be screened out of the book. The editor, his sensibility made more quickly articulate by virtue of his having worked out the axiom, should be of help at the screening.

The editor then asks a question straight from the craft book: What moved your mother to characteristic action? What appetites did she *act for,* and what gads would she *react to?*

"She wanted *position* in the town. This meant some money, so she badgered Father for that. What she really wanted was to hold a salon, be the intellectual and cultural duchess of the county. She was this strange combination of confidence and paranoia. She despised weakness. She was militantly on guard against disgrace. It was only years later I learned that her own father was convicted of something like embezzlement, though he got a suspended sentence. He had to report to a parole officer for five years. After that they moved out of state. Her mother became an alcoholic. She—my mother—had a n'er-do-well brother she didn't see for twenty years. There's more, but in any case when she married my father and moved to [call it 'Carlisle'] she had dreams. The town had been *named* after my father's family. When, for reasons, he finally committed suicide, she didn't feel grieved or guilty, she just felt angry. This was disgrace squared. Everyone figured she drove him to do it. She and I quarreled, and my brother Ross. We both left home."

Did she drive him to it?

"Yes, I suppose, but not as directly as people thought. He *was* weak, he *couldn't* run the mill, the family business. But there was something else, it's unclear. Turns out he'd been having an affair with a local girl and it went bad somehow. It also turns out my mother had something going with someone important in Macon, I never could get the details. But someone not weak, not feckless, and they all bumped into each other in a hotel in Atlanta. Marvelous imbroglio, I think."

You 'think'?

"I'm making this up as I go along. You made me think about it, and I can see her own life was actually shapeless. Nothing really happened in it. But this *potential* was there. Given the right ingredients in her life, this *could* have happened."

So a biographically accurate account won't do what you want to do.

"Well, no. It *is* a novel, after all. What's art *about*, anyway? Shaping material. I can honestly feel that, re-shaped, it's even truer. A straight chronicle, even if it could detail every hour of her waking life, which it couldn't, probably wouldn't convey the feeling of life with her. It's like dialogue. In my imagination I can hear her say things that she never actually *did* say, but that *get her across* better than most of the true-life lines of hers that I *can* recall."

Her ultimate master-prelibation: "I want the reader to feel what she was like—appreciate her brains, charm, and drive; her discontent and callousness; her blindness; I want him to sense what it felt like to be in her magnetic field; I want to catch him up in the accelerating rush to the crash, the increasingly radical gambles, that her dreams—given the right situation—were bound to produce." This is what she wants the reader to *experience*. This was her sought-for master-prelibation—or, rather, its verbal expression, its axiom—and it was arrived at through a discussion that the editor was pursuing in order to frame an axiom. The conversation served as a hothouse that sped the ripening of her thoughts and feelings about what she wanted the book to do. Now she could better divine an applicable somacluster and apposite accident.

That story calls to mind a popular novel of a few years ago that could have yielded an axiom like this: "She could not stand 'mess' in her life, probably because of the humiliation her own parents caused her. So when her son tried to commit suicide, her reaction was not concern but anger, and fear for image in the community. I want the reader to see her as she acted on these motivations, and to feel their impact not just on her son but on her husband, and understand how his new perception of how misdirected, cold, and unforgiving she basically was, stopped her husband's love. The reader should also feel the boy's guilt and his struggle to work it through. It should feel inevitable when the mother simply goes away.''

Notice it says nothing explicit about the story's lesson or 'meaning', though the reader is free to generalize if he will.

I said that the axiom for a novel that initiated with a lesson or insight must give instruction about emotions and attitudes and whom to attach them to, or no one will care about the message.

But a novel in which the writer's aim is initially to convey an emotional experience need not be labeled with any specific message. "I want my reader to feel the soul-ripping experience of having a four-year-old child who gets cancer and takes two years to die. I know that academics may declare the theme to be 'life is unfair' or 'love endures all' or some other damn platitude, and teach students that's what I wanted to 'say' or that's the 'meaning' of the book and why I wrote it. But they'll be wrong. Why can't they see that a novelist's first intent, what she wants the reader to come away with, is a *feeling.* If I thought my readers got from my novel only an aphorism, I'd think the book was a failure."

When the effect-wanted is an emotional experience, think of the axiom as a tuning fork: It does not test the melody; it tells if each note is on key.

It's worth rephrasing this warning to writers (and to editors inclined to coerce the writer into expressing his axiom too early): *Starting* with the message as an axiom has dangers beyond the one of its tending to prompt a writer to create merely utilitarian characters. It can stifle unimplied prelibation.

Master-prelibation is best kept above a certain altitude, not lowering like Big Brother. The axiom may be pinned to the bulletin board, but it mustn't glare at the writer, blinking like a stop sign. It should be there, available like a road map when wanted, but many writers emphasize the importance of being open to the unexpected call. Regular prelibations should be subordinate to the master-prelibation, but they do need freedom to breathe, to get on with their job, even, sometimes, to go into the boss's office and suggest a new goal entirely. In the end, as Auchincloss suggests, if their rebellion doesn't work, they can always be taken out and shot.

Writers, even those who start with more in hand than Doctorow and Didion, often will testify that they have to write much or all of a first draft before they gain any surety of what the book ought to do, what its master-effect should be.

Even when the initium and congruent emerging master-prelibation is a sensational experience, merely planning those sensations, and restricting the axiom to *that*, will not be enough.

"I want him to feel what it's like to be in the jungle: the heat, the constant sense of threat, the fatigue, the multiplicity of factors impinging on Juan every time he has to make a survival decision. In other words, it should feel like an adventure." But—and this does not actually go without saying, though you might expect it to do so—the author must design and cause the *attitude* he needs: "I also want him to like Juan so he roots for him to survive; and, by the end, the reader should admire Juan for his bravery and resourcefulness." None of this says a word about the specific gads Juan should be subjected to, but clearly the general requirement is that they should be life-threatening much of the time, and demanding bravery or ingenuity all the time. So don't have him spend hours worrying about his appearance. It also requires the writer to fight off the impulse to fill the pages with flashbacks explaining Juan's history, as he hacks through the underbrush. Flashbacks will take us out of the jungle, the heat will fade, the threat, the fatigue. "But I want the reader to know who Juan *is!*" Okay, says the axiom, but the way you phrased me said your first interest was in conveying the intensity of his adventure. Flashbacks vitiate that. Tell us who he is, quickly, before his trek starts. If the book is intended to be a sociological portrait of the first Puerto Rican fighter pilot, it should be set back home and in flight school, not in the jungle.

Yes, a fleeting thought about the girl he left behind could contribute, but this writer's prelibations should constantly be focused on new kinds of jungle sensations, tests, and excitements for imagination to render concrete. To the extent that Juan himself is credibly seized by reverie and delirium, some flashback can be okay; but if it's merely an expository author tediously pursuing a misplaced drive to 'fill us in', it's likely to harm rather than enhance.

The kinds of functions I've been saying should be designed into the axiom apply no matter what level of orthodox narrative fiction is being attempted. Everyone, from category romance writers to Umberto Eco and Anne Tyler, must be concerned with a novel's coalescence, with its freedom from harmful distractions (and from harmful restrictions), with its feel of and focus on activity, with the emotion, attitude, insight wanted within the reader during and after the read—with, in other words, effecting the master-prelibation.

Some writers press themselves through to a clear master-prelibation before they put a word of the novel itself on paper. Others have to mount whole drafts of exploration, sightseeing, surveying, before they know what they want to do.

Still others have testified they have finished books in a single draft, drawn forward by a homing instinct they could not define, explain, or predict, unaware of their destination, until one day they just arrived, they were done and they knew it.

But it is not given to most writers to write that way.

The usual process is to think and feel their way from initium through to their master-prelibation, the monitor from above that then starts, or reorganizes, the march of prelibations on the ground. These in their turn select the characters, circuitry, setting, and gads of circumstance, the accidents, and the point and voice of view—the substance and tone of narrative. Thus is a novel conceived, gestated, and born.

These remarks about axiom are unfinished because, in truth, my thoughts about it—and about everything else in this book—are unfinished too. For example, a suppressed premise of my argument for axiom is that the author's master-prelibation, his intuition about the effect that the book as a whole could and should have, can be brought from mere vapor form down through liquid to a persevering solid, something he can lean on. And yet I'm certain that this possibility varies with the mind of the writer. There are those for whom the master-prelibation will never get harder than, say, runny gelatin.

Generally speaking, this is a disadvantage. Generally, but not always. For some writers, a certain fluidity of purpose and a readiness to go with the flow are essential to the vitality and freshness of their writing. So the question about them is not only *can* their purpose be solidified, but *should* it? Evidently not. But who is "them"?

For example, I personally am absentminded. I can arrive in the other room and forget why I went there. I can think of something I must do, and the very thought sometimes flicks in my mind as though I'd done the thing—so I forget to do it. I'm regularly starting a second thing before the first thing is done.

I have no illusions that this is because I am preoccupied with great concepts. I know it for what it is—a species of stupidity.

A head like that needs guide ropes, buzzers, devices to supplement the persevering fixity of aim it is weak in.

For a head like that, axioms sound like a good thing.

That problem, "I forgot what I was doing," is different from "I never figured out what I was doing."

The second problem could also be alleviated by working on axioms.

I don't mean my problem is *similar* to one that handicaps certain writers; I say it is *identical:* I as a writer often find myself rabbiting off course to nibble in harebrained ecstasy at some irrelevant fern of thought. In every creative pursuit—philosophy, science, art—such excursions have been known, on rare occasion, to be fruitful. Usually, though, when the rabbit finally looks up, it is dusk and he is far from home, and he hears a symbolic owl's hoot. Most writers who have these failings had better find ways to cope with them or they'll never get home at all.

For this kind of 'them', pushing through to axiom doesn't kill vitality, it supports it.

The trick for the editor is to discern what kind of writer he has on his hands. If it's the first kind, perhaps the editor should carefully confine his eliciting queries to concrete matters in the narrative—character, relationships between them, the circumstantial pressures on them. But what if hyperemia sets in? What if the 'flow' becomes a chaotic drift? If the novel courses so far off its original canvas that no reader's mind can any longer find a frame for it, should the editor simply wave it good-bye? Or does he try to deflect it back? When should he judge he is no longer the *right* editor for this book?

I may say that the clang of metallic doors and the sound of approaching voices force me to leave these matters unresolved, but I know such thoughts will always be less than final. My first motive in this book has been the conviction that we must at least get started.

A x i n g   T h e m e

In the essay I said that the concept of 'theme' was malignantly balled up. Part of the support for this doleful
conclusion came from the examination of nineteen of the
leading textbooks of the last two decades, volumes that
announced themselves as introductions to literature and
its writing, and that talked about theme. I'll quote from
several of them in this Note. There have been texts—and
new ones arise each year—that avoid the term 'theme'
entirely, but the ones I inspected comprised, statistically,
the huge majority of the instructionals assigned to under-
graduates in our colleges in recent times.

Let's start calmly: Samples of the way 'theme' is
taught should be sent to Atlanta so the Centers for Dis-
ease Control can get on it; the NIH should be called in,
and a "Just Say No to 'Theme'" campaign should be
promulgated among the youth of America. (The French
have already volunteered their help, but they have succeeded only in introducing a second virus.)

In flat: The way 'theme' is currently taught is actively
harmful.

I seriously pursue this crusade here, albeit in con-
densed, almost outline, form, because I believe that
what's being done in classrooms stunts, and even kills,
the ability and appetite of many of the best students. This
deprives our globe of much talent that would otherwise
find itself in writing, teaching, reading . . . and editing.

Their teaching of 'theme' is harmful because of what
it leads *to,* and what it leads *away from.*

In the student's mood and attitude, it leads to confusion, discouragement, and alienation.

In his knowledge it leads to error about what authors are trying to do, and about what is cherishable in fiction generally, and stories and novels individually.

It leads the student away from enjoyment, sanguine expectation, and trust in literature. It actually *reduces* the possibility of his focusing where the reward is.

It does this by forcibly thrusting on the student a concept that is fuzzy, arbitrary, trivializing, irrelevant, distracting, and ultimately deadening.

It's important to realize that this enforcement is executed by a figure who has immense authoritative ascendancy over the students. The student (initially) respects, trusts and obeys him. The more dedicated the student already is to reading, the more devoted he is to the idea of studying under the great professor, the man who *sees*, and *knows*, and who will convey the keys to appreciating great writers and great books. Because the professor is both lofty and wrong, the result is either sore disillusionment and withdrawal, or a kind of lobotomy, the disconnection of sensibility, replacing it with a soulless response and printout worthy of a microchip.

To understand why this happens, we should first get down the definition of 'theme' that is generally taught. (We could begin by comparing the contradictions among texts—"The theme is the moral"; "The theme is never the moral"; "The theme is the subject"; "The theme is never the subject"—but each author would, justifiably, claim he should not be held responsible for what other authors say. Still, the point that there *are* disputes is worth mentioning for students' benefit, because the young mind confronting any textbook tends to accept it as factual, like a primer in history or mathematics. I'll content myself in a moment with noting the contradictions *within* texts.)

At first hearing, the notion sounds benign. The 'theme' of a work is said to be (Perrine:)* "its controlling idea or its central insight"; (Hall:) "a central insight into human experience"; (Pickering:) "the central idea or statement about life that unifies and controls the work"; (Trimmer:) "the central and unifying idea about human experience"; (Gordon:) "the main idea, the abstract statement of what the work means, its significance . . . central meaning"; (Kane:) "the central meaning."

Its benignity begins to fade a bit as the student starts to realize he's having trouble grasping the thing. He's not sure what 'meaning' means here; or 'idea'; or 'significance'. . . .

So the authors go on, aiming to clarify things, and the dominant tack is to emphasize that the student arrives at the theme by *generalizing,* producing a general *statement* about the human condition as implied by the total story. (Perrine:) "It is the unifying generalization about life stated or implied by the story"; (Hall:) "the implicit generality the story supports . . . we express the theme by a sentence or two of generalization"; (Pickering:) "[Sometimes] theme is tied to a revelation of character and takes the form of a statement about that character and what the fate of that character may imply about people or life in general"; (Gordon:) "The statement of what a story means should be a general one,

---

*See source references at the end of this Note.

applying not only to the story, but also showing its rela-
tion to life"; (Brooks:) "not only an evaluation of the
particular experience related in the story, but a *generalized*
evaluation. Always the end of a successful story leaves us
with an attitude to take toward life in general."

The student seldom realizes it, but by this point he
has already been deflected away from delight and understanding. But, innocent and eager, he presses on with his
assignment: to derive a generalization about "life in general" from the particulars of the story.

Quite naturally, his first efforts tend to be in the form
of a 'moral'.

No, no, he's told; you're confused; a theme is not a
moral; that's not the kind of generalization about life we
meant. (Pickering:) "To identify the theme [as] 'crime
doesn't pay' is to confuse theme with moral"; (Kane:)
"Theme should not be confused with moral, a simple tag
which can be abstracted as the 'point' of a narrative."

The student's eyes begin to blink; evidently there's
a difference between the 'purpose' and the 'point' of a
narrative.

My main point (or purpose) right here is not to stress
the *confusion* 'theme' causes so much as the *distraction;* still
it's worthwhile to exhibit these lines from Perrine bear-
ing on 'moral':

"The theme is the purpose of the story."

"The purpose is not to inculcate a code of moral
rules."

"Occasionally the theme may be expressed as a
moral principle."

So theme equals purpose, purpose is *not* moral, but
theme can be moral.

It turns out that what Perrine is against is not a moral but the pursuit by the student for a moral, the "trying to wring from every story a didactic pronouncement about life." This, Perrine warns, tends to reduce the story "to some dusty platitude." Somehow it should be a "central generalization about life" without being a "didactic pronouncement about life."

By now the student is bobbing his head, open-mouthed, apparently rapt, while sneaking a glance to his left to see if the guy next to him is getting something he's not.

Three more instructions about theme are usually put to him in these textbooks:

1. Theme should be in the form of a statement, a sentence. Not 'the futility of envy' but 'Envy is futile.'
2. The theme must 'account for', 'explain', all the major details of the story.
3. Perrine: "We should avoid any statement that reduces the theme to some familiar saying." Perrine claims his point is that quick settlement for an old verbal formula probably cuts the sharp corners off and "impoverishes the central meaning of the story."

The student is beginning to learn something, not about literature, but about classroom tactics. Avoid the word 'moral'. Convert all imperatives into declaratives. Make sure the theme is phrased so it's not recognizable as a cliché. Cynicism, which is the correct response to manipulation, stirs.

'Theme' is not an incisor, it is a molar, and now we're getting close to the nerve. The touchy center of the issue is: When the student finally picks his delicate, unsure, trepid way through to what the professor will accept as the 'theme', what's he got? Perrine has not given the full reason for professorial jitteriness about commonplace themes.

Here is a selection of 'themes' as phrased by the authors of those textbooks:

(Perrine:) "War is horrible." "Old age is often pathetic and in need of understanding." "Motherhood sometimes has more frustrations than rewards." "Loyalty to country often inspires heroic self-sacrifice." "In springtime there occasionally comes to those upper-middle-class people whose lives are bound by respectability and regulated by conventions a peculiar impulse toward life, freedom and beauty; but the impulse is seldom strong enough to overcome the deep-seated forces of habit and convention." "The soul of every man is mysterious in its origins and contains unfathomed possibilities for evil and violence as well as for innocence and love." "The love of two people for each other is a more worthwhile object of desire than business success or financial prosperity." "The theme of *Othello* may be expressed as 'Jealousy exacts a terrible cost'."

(Trimmer:) "Nature is not cruel; it is indifferent."

(Gordon:) "People fooled twice may not respond a third time." "Don't call for help unless you need it." "Death is the only ending for one who will accept no social responsibilities." "A man cannot control fate by supernatural means."

(Roberts:) "Human beings who are committed to caring for others may actually suffer for this commitment." "Even if a commitment to the dead is strong, the commitment to life is stronger." "The love of a man and a woman is so positive that it can literally rescue people from death." "Selfless love may lead to bravery against hopeless odds." "Women, with no power except their charm and beauty, are helpless against chance and bad luck." "Racial barriers separate human beings and make them cruel when it would be to everyone's interest to unite and to be helpful." [On *Hamlet*] "A person doing evil sets strong forces in motion that cannot be stopped until everything in the person's path is destroyed."

(Abcarian:) [On *The Secret Sharer*] "The recognition of complex moral ambiguities is essential to maturity."

(Barnet:) "Life and love are too strong to be buried alive." "the quest for happiness"; "the difficulty of achieving self-knowledge"; "the fragility of love." [Notice these last are not in statement form.]

(Packer:) "Frustrated desire in Emily Brontë's *Wuthering Heights*, obsession in Herman Melville's *Moby Dick.*"

Hall expresses the theme of Chekhov's 'Gooseberries' this way: "People deceive themselves." Then an instinct I'll leave you to name prompts him to add: "And their overriding purposes distort their perceptions of reality." What he adds is syllables.

While you ponder the depth, freshness, illumination, utility, and value of all these expressions, listen to these authors on the importance here:

(Hall:) "A story's theme is its reason for being."

(Perrine:) "Theme is the purpose of the story."

(Packer:) "The theme is the point or meaning."

(Brooks:) "The theme is what a piece of fiction stacks up to . . . the significance."

I now submit that, given the themes expressed above, to teach young people that these are the reasons

for the stories' being; that they were the purpose, meaning, and significance for Shakespeare, Chekhov, Welty, et
al.; and that they are what students must struggle to get
out of them—this is a lesson of such mind-imploding
fatuity as to amount to assault with a deadly weapon.

Ah, the protest will come, you obviously haven't read
us closely. We regularly admit that a theme is a poor,
inadequate thing next to the work itself.

But I *have* read you closely, as closely as, I fear,
countless bewildered students have, young minds who
will feel there's something wrong with *them* that they
cannot reconcile the contradictory things they are hearing.

When Pickering says, "One of the marks of a great
work of literature—a work that we generally regard as a
'classic'—is the significance of its theme," he is not let off
the hook by saying two pages later, "The ideas that constitute a work's theme may be relatively commonplace."

When Perrine says, "Theme is the purpose of the
story," he does not insulate himself from indictment by
saying just four paragraphs later, "We must never think,
once we have stated the theme of a story, the whole
purpose of the story has been to yield up this abstract
statement."

When Perrine advances the themes ascribed to him
above ("War is horrible", etc.), and we begin to frown,
should our brow smooth over because he then double-
speaks that one should abhor "dusty platitudes"?

To the student pertinacious enough to bring into
juxtaposition statements that Perrine separately makes
over the seven pages of his essay on theme, Perrine continually seems to want it both ways:

"Story writers' first business is to reveal life."

"A story's *first* object is enjoyment."

"Theme exists when an author has deliberately introduced some concept or theory of life that the story is meant to illustrate."

"Good writers do not ordinarily write a story to 'illustrate' a theme."

"Occasionally the theme is a moral principle."

"A story is not a preachment."

When Perrine says writers are "wary of spoiling a story for perceptive readers by 'explaining' it as some people ruin jokes by explaining them," it doesn't occur to him that students may ask: "Then why ask *me* to do it?" and that the instinct behind their question may not be laziness but indeed a suspicion that there is something ruinous in this. (If I seem prolongedly mean about Perrine, one of my reasons for dwelling on him is precisely the reason why he can ignore and survive my gnatish attention: His book, I'm told, has been assigned to more college literature students than any other text for at least the past fifteen years.)

Many of the textbooks' authors at last admit that the long fuse of theme-pursuit leads, in the end, to a dud.

We've noted Pickering conceding that "a work's theme may be relatively commonplace."

(Hall:) "Simple summaries of theme are not adequate to describe great short stories."

(Kane:) "Theme-statement is inevitably an oversimplification."

(Heffernan:) "Most attempts to expound *the* theme of a story will leave us with a sense of dissatisfaction and

incompleteness. A good story resists a convenient sum-
mation. When 'boiled down' to simple statements, the
themes of most stories will not seem profound."

Even Perrine: "The bare statement of the theme, so
lifeless and impoverished when abstracted from the
story, may seem to diminish the story to something less
than it is. This dry statement is a poor thing beside the
living reality of the story."

The student, baffled, discouraged, sensing himself
being robbed of the enjoyment he used to get from
books, and feeling he has drifted from a literature class
into one of those disembodying philosophy classes his
mother warned him against, growls as he packs his bag.
"Then why make us hunt for theme at all?" He is now on
the edge of articulating an astonishing problem that
none of the nineteen texts faces up to:

Never, despite their brief, abortive invocation of 'significance', *do they show any correlation whatever between the
quality of theme and the quality of the story.* Hall staggers into
the subject and, with evident unwit, comes out on the
wrong side: "Theme requires our attention because it is
a story's reason for being. Not all stories have themes
[e.g., Poe's 'Murders in the Rue Morgue']." (Wait! the
student cries. That means . . . what does that mean? That
Poe's story had no reason for being? What's 'reason'
mean here? No motive for Poe's writing it? or no justification for Hall's tolerating its existence?) Don't worry;
Hall will clear things up: 'Morgue' has no theme because
"it will not lead to an insight into human character."
(Wait! Is this a defining factor in 'theme'? What consti-
tutes such an 'insight'?) "Generally, stories without
themes are inferior art. They can be well-written and

pleasing, but they lack seriousness." (But suppose the 'insight' is a banality?) Don't worry; Hall continues to clear things up: "On the other hand, not all stories with themes are serious works of art. Many popular stories develop commonplace or trite themes." Now the student says more than "Wait!" He yells to Hall, "Stop and turn around! You just gave the theme to Chekhov's 'Gooseberries' as 'People deceive themselves.' This 'insight' is quintessentially trite. And yet Sean O'Faolain could say, 'I think Chekhov's "Gooseberries" is the best short story ever written.' Something's wrong here. The theme is the story's reason for being, and yet there can be stories with no themes. 'Theme' requires 'insight'. But the insight can be a stunning platitude! So what good is the insight, and therefore what good is *theme* if there is effectively no correlation between its merit and the merit of the story?"

But Hall has not stopped and turned around. He has wobbled blandly on: "When you read a propaganda story, be wary of approving the fiction just because you agree with the politics. Don't swallow bad art for the sake of worthy ideas." Which really tears it finally: You can evidently have a terrific, noble, original 'theme' and a story that's bad art.

So if trite themes can beget great art, and great themes can beget trite art, and no theme at all can beget Poe, what the hell use is this vivisecting hunt for theme?

(A corollary: There must be ten thousand stories that, to a professor, would yield the theme 'People deceive themselves.' Ninety-nine percent of those stories are justifiably forgotten. But if theme is the significance of the story, why aren't all these stories equally significant? Because the professors are wrong in their teaching:

The significance, the purpose, the meaning, the reason for being of a story does *not* lie in its 'theme' but in something else.)

The authors have yet another rearguard answer at the ready: In the pursuit of theme, it's not the destination that counts, but the journey.

(Pickering:) "It forces us to bring together and to understand the various aspects of the work; in this process we may notice things we had previously ignored or undervalued. The identification of theme, then, is a way to validate our understanding, to focus our response."

(Trimmer:) "Sends us back to the story itself to reexamine our thinking about its central idea."

(Hall:) "Reassures us that we are all reading the same story."

(Perrine:) "Reveals to us aspects of a story that we should otherwise not have noticed and will thereby lead to more thorough understanding. The ability to state theme, moreover, is a test of our understanding."

Perrine is dead wrong again. If a student reads *Othello,* and Perrine asks him to state the theme, and the student gives Perrine's answer, "Jealousy exacts a terrible cost," that may prove to *Perrine* that the student 'understands' *Othello,* but it wouldn't prove it to me.

The motivation of these authors, to get the student to pay close attention, to focus, is a good one. Their technique, a search for 'theme', is a bad one. Because it makes the student attend to the wrong thing, it focuses him in the wrong way.

Flannery O'Connor: "People talk about the theme of a story as if the theme were like a string that a sack of chicken feed is tied with. They think that if you can pick out the theme, the way you pick the right thread in the chicken-feed sack, you can rip the story open and feed the chickens. But this is not the way meaning works in fiction. . . . The meaning of a story has to be embodied in it, has to be made concrete in it. A story is a way to say something that can't be said any other way, and it takes every word in the story to say what the meaning is."

(Amazingly, Pickering quotes this with approval, then goes on to give five suggestions for identifying theme, "the abstract, generalized statement or comment that the work makes." And this man is teaching our children how to read?)

O'Connor is saying categorically that her 'meaning' cannot be conveyed in any abstract statement. Her 'central insight', her 'purpose', the reason for her story's being is *not* a generalized statement about life, and to lead students into looking for it that way is to *mis*lead them. O'Connor does have a 'central meaning', and it's something like this: What you get when you go after the piece of string is a piece of string, not my feed; if I wanted to convey a nonfiction generalized abstraction I could write my own essay.

Susan Sontag: "By reducing art to its content and then interpreting *that,* one tames the work of art. . . . This philistinism of interpretation is more rife in literature than in any other art. . . . Interpretation, based on the highly dubious theory that a work of art is composed of items of content, violates art. . . . The function of criticism should be to show *how it is what it is,* even *that it is what it is,* rather than show *what it means.*"

The charge before the court has been that the way 'theme' is taught confuses, discourages, and alienates students; that it misleads them about what authors are trying to do, and about what is to be enjoyed and cherished in literature; and that it actively *reduces* the possibility of their focusing on what's valuable in a literary work.

I hope the case has been made that the alert student, confronted with such lazy, irrational, and irrelevant nonsense as we've seen, has grounds for saying at last, "The hell with this," and walking away. (An alarming corollary: The students who endure and even embrace this inanity, and who are thus allowed to go on through advanced degrees to become the next generation of professors and textbook writers, are likely to be precisely the *wrong* sort of teachers of literature in the future.)

And I think it's safe to say that the immense majority of published writers would join O'Connor in saying that the 'theme' tack won't even come close to causing students to put their focus where the writer would like them to.

We can paraphrase the expressed sentiments of certain other authors: "I wanted to convey what it was like to be in that jungle war, what it felt like to be under fire, and how it brought out different things in different men. My 'meaning' was not 'war is hell'; some men did not find it so, or not in the same way. It degraded some men, but I saw others sober up, actually take on a strength and decency. But my 'meaning' certainly wasn't that men differ, or that extreme pressure reveals the true man. I didn't write the book to convey a two-cent platitude like that. What I wanted was for the reader to *be there,* to experience. A novel shouldn't have to reduce to one general truth; most of the best books I've read seem to contain a thousand truths."

Grinding my own axiom, I'd say that what guided a writer like this one was not a "unifying generalization about life", but a master-effect-wanted.

"I feel despair every time I think of some pundit saying that the theme of my book is that being widowed teaches such and such—the unfairness of life, the guilt the survivor feels, something like that. As I wrote the book I had no ulterior agenda; I was constantly seized only with the need to make the reader feel and understand what my so-called heroine was going through. That's why I chose the POV I did. It did involve guilt and rage, but it also involved lots of other things that I felt profoundly but for which I could never think of any words except the way I told the story in the book. If there was anything like a 'purpose' beyond that, it was to say to a lot of people out there, 'You are not alone.' "

Now hear a robust, literary athlete whose novels always feature a compelling story that thunders on like a boulder down a mountain, bowling irrelevancies out of the way; he's a professional curmudgeon who jeers at theme (and would jeer at axiom if led to it): "Theme is spurious merchandise hawked by camp followers. I just tell my story; let the tweedy clerics in elbow patches invent its 'meaning'. They have to do that because if a preacher's got no enlightenment to sell he doesn't get dinner."

Of course, I would claim even this curmudgeon is guided by a master-prelibation that's so strong he never has to put it into an axiom as a clarifier and reminder—

though if I said so he'd just laugh genially and dump his whiskey in my lap. And I would further claim that a student of his work would profit from a detailed examination of just how he gets the effects he does. But I would *not* claim there was any adult benefit in trying to extract a generality that "leaves us with an attitude to take toward life in general."

The remaining counts in the indictment—that the professors' 'theme' hunt misleads the student about, indeed positively shields him from, a good book's best reward—is something that would be corroborated by many adults looking back on their school days. Picture the student, told that he must derive an abstract generality that "accounts for" and "explains" all the major details of a story. He figuratively dons his white clinician's smock and knuckles down to his grim task. He lays the tale out on a slab and begins his joyless dissections—not in search of its beauty of feature, grace of movement, charm of voice, vitality of nature, but in search of its 'idea'; in search not of its feeling but of its 'statement'; not of what it does, but of what it 'says'.

When he has finished his examination, he then must write up his report, a tricky business requiring that all the x's, y's, and z's be encompassed in the algebraic formula. In the end it no more conveys the meaning of what's on the slab than the coroner's report that starts, "A well-nourished Caucasian female of one hundred eighteen pounds, aged between twenty-five and thirty . . ."

But at last he's completed his assignments. It took concentration. He had to lay aside a lot of distracting flesh, but he's done it, he's found the theme and extracted it. He's written it up. I'm finished with this one, thank God, now I can go home.

Anecdote: Many years ago, when I was taking a writing class in college, an extraordinarily shy fellow student wrote a story in which the climactic moment had the heroine on a horse in dense woods. She bids the horse to jump a hurdle of obscuring brush and he will not do it. She is agitated, he is adamant, during a subtly Lawrentian battle of wills. At last the woman gets off the horse and exasperatedly pokes through the brush—to discover a hundred-foot drop onto railroad tracks. I can only tell you that the story, which was admittedly lacking in adult polish, had an eerie, dark intimacy—as many of D. H. Lawrence's own stories do. But the instructor wanted something else. "What are you *saying*?" he badgered. "What is the story *saying*?" The wretched girl stood rigid at the front of the class, voiceless, violated, staring at her hands as the instructor reached the point of chuckling at her. "What are you *saying*? That animals are smarter than people?" And he laughed out loud. At last she raised her head and turned her eyes on him in one of the most final looks I've ever seen. "Yes," she said, and she walked out of the classroom and we never saw her again.

I've conceded that the goal of getting the reader to pay closer attention is a good one. The assumption of the professors is that, by compelling the student to crawl back over the narrative in the effort to ensure that all the 'major details' are 'accounted for' by the theme, one forces the student to focus on each scene, each character, every element in the book. But I've argued that, because during this crawl his focus is kept on the thin, flat, ideational plane, he's likely to miss the essential lovable things, like a chemist analyzing the molecular structure of different ice creams. It calls to mind the old days when history teachers figured that they'd do the job by compelling students to memorize a thousand names and dates.

But at least the chemist and historian inculcate some facts that may ultimately have some narrow use. The English professor in the end abandons that claim. He knows that themes like 'People deceive themselves' and 'Jealousy exacts a terrible cost' are indefensibly meager payoffs.

Now, having dismissed theme as an end and also as a pedogogic means, it would seem meet for me to suggest an alternative technique. The technique should serve to get the student to pay the closer attention I approve of, but also to ensure that the focus is brought to bear where the true reward is.

The approach I'd recommend is based on two things. The first is the schema of art described in the essay, in which I say that the first stage is prelibation—an intuition of an effect-wanted—followed by imagination's conjuring of narrative to produce that effect, and then by sensibility's judgments on those conjurings. This maintains that the aim of the artist is to produce an effect on the reader's head, heart, or gut.

The second is my own experience that the most rewarding critics for me, over the years, have been those who often do no more than *point*. When Cowley says to me, just go back and read the list of people who attended Gatsby's party, just savor how Fitzgerald describes them, it'll be worth it—he does me a profound service. If a great appreciator like Cowley tells me it will be worth it, just for itself, and not because it's necessary as step #7 in the derivation of an abstract generality, the very freedom from ulterior function enhances vision. To see the true color of the painting, do not wear glasses tinted with other intent. Sontag was right.

But then I must back down a bit and concede this teaching can't be done solely with the index finger.

What I recommend, then, is approaching the work of fiction with a program of questions devised to focus the reader on the effect achieved, and how the author achieved it.

For example, each character has a certain impact on us, the readers. To clarify how that impact is achieved, certainly notice what he says and does, what we're told about him; even ask crafty questions: What does he want or promise? What does he do to get it? What result does he cause? Why do we like or dislike him?

Move on to circuitry: How does he braid or conflict with others in the cast?

Look at circumstance; notice the gads, and how they plug into gad-receptors.

Then, really to clarify the appreciation of effects on us, and how the author is causing them, the gifted instructor, as rare teachers through the ages have when they were not fouled in the lines of theme, might bid his most gifted students to ask: *How would the story and our response be different if such-and-such were different?*

The instructor might help students to imagine a character different, or missing entirely. What happens to the circuitry? Imagine what would be the story-effect of a new character: Hamlet's sister.

Examine each scene. First ask: Do we like it? Then ask: Why? The answer to this question always takes the form, ultimately, of simply pointing at things and taking a stand: I love this sentence; I love what she says, what he does; I think this description is great.

Sometimes crafty, gridlike questions about the scene help us push below the general pleasure to the specific credit in the narrative. How does the scene reveal or change character, circuitry, or circumstance? Are things different at the end of the scene from how they were at the beginning? How much of the vital feeling stems from this advancement, from our observation that something is really *going on,* things are *happening?* Always the aim is to notice the effect on us, the readers, as we contemplate each element of the narrative, notice the gustant plea- sures each gives, the salivancies generated and *how* they're generated. (How different would we feel if this tease, hint, threat, possibility were never introduced?)

This appreciation can be applied on a page-to-page level; at book's end, as we consider its total effect, the same questions, or some new questions of the same sort, arise. To raise your appreciation of the book *as is,* ask: How would we have felt about it if Fitzgerald had Daisy leave Tom and run off forever with Gatsby? Suppose we conjecture something about FSF's *master-prelibation?* If we try to articulate it, work up its verbal expression, the *axiom,* would it really differ from a professor's *theme?* Try it. It would.

The themes that academia has advanced for *The Great Gatsby* take forms like these: "You cannot recover the past." "The great American Dream has failed." "The pursuit of false gods leads to destruction."

Academia may publicly abjure 'morals', but (as the newly cynical student perceives) the majority of profes- sors' themes *are* morals, albeit in the disguise of declara- tive generalities.

The axiom takes a form that may or may not include a reminder of what the author wants the reader to *see,* but it certainly includes what he wants the reader to *feel.* Fitzgerald wanted the reader to feel, among other things, the difference between the American aristocracy—that is, those raised on vintage, respectable money—and those who weren't, and the unbridgeable gap between the two. He wanted to convey the permeance of those two backgrounds, how Daisy's very voice had "the sound of money" in it. But it was more than that. Respectable money brought with it a callous regal presumption that the plebeians were there to be utilities, you were polite to them, you treated them awfully well, of course, but we know what they *are* after all, don't we? You could seduce them, but love them? Feel them as equals? Well, the way you could love a good servant or a good horse, maybe. But sit down to dinner with a horse?

And FSF wanted the reader to feel that paradoxically seductive power as it cast its spell on the plebeian. Jay Gatsby, born James Gatz, is hypnotized by Daisy's aristocratic, golden-girl aura. How could that be, a hard-headed gangster like him, sappy romantic about this feather-light girl? But it's precisely one of FSF's aims to convince you, to make you feel and believe in the spell. And to make you feel that a total marriage of true minds can never be, between those classes. Jay could never, in the end, get Daisy away.

I'm aware that all this, and more that FSF wanted to effect in his readers, can be reduced to declarative sentences about such things as the instinctive presumptions of the rich and the emotional thralldom of the un-anointed, and I don't claim he would say all such sentences were false. But he would not say they were the truth; a cerebral generality was not the truth he was after. The truth was how these things *felt*. The heart has its reasons, and they are not embodied in a sociologist's line.

And thus his axiom would be shaped for, and aimed at, something deeper than the cortex.

The professors accept 'Jealousy exacts a terrible cost' as the theme of *Othello*. Would Shakespeare have accepted it as his axiom?

SOURCES

Abcarian, Richard, and Marvin Klotz. *Literature the Human Experience.* New York: St. Martin's Press, 1984.

Barnet, Sylvan, Morton Berman, and William Burto. *An Introduction to Literature.* Boston: Little, Brown, 1977.

Brooks, Cleanth, and Robert Penn Warren. *Understanding Fiction.* Englewood Cliffs, N.J.: Prentice-Hall, 1979.

Gordon, Edward J. *Writing About Imaginative Literature.* New York: Harcourt Brace Jovanovich, 1973.

Hall, Donald. *To Read Literature: Fiction Poetry Drama.* New York: Holt, Rinehart and Winston, 1983.

Heffernan, William A., Mark Johnston, and Frank Hodgins. *Literature: Art and Artifact.* San Diego: Harcourt Brace Jovanovich, 1987.

Kane, Thomas S., and Leonard J. Peters. *The Short Story and the Reader: Discovering Narrative Techniques.* Oxford, England: Oxford University Press, 1976.

Packer, Nancy Huddleston, and John Timpane. *Writing Worth Reading: A Practical Guide.* New York: St. Martin's Press, 1986.

Perrine, Laurence, and Thomas R. Arp. *Literature: Structure, Sound, and Sense.* San Diego: Harcourt Brace Jovanovich, 1983.

Pickering, James H., and Jeffrey D. Hoeper. *Literature.* New York: Macmillan, 1986.

Roberts, Edgar V., and Henry E. Jacobs. *Literature: An Introduction to Reading and Writing.* Englewood Cliffs, N.J.: Prentice-Hall, 1986.

Trimmer, Joseph F., and C. Wade Jennings. *Fictions.* San Diego: Harcourt Brace Jovanovich, 1985.

Music Appreciation

There is an analogy, perhaps, in a demanding course in music analysis and appreciation. "Notice the oboe counterpoint here; isolate in your ear just the flute; see what he's doing with it?" It won't teach you how to compose ingeniously, but you will compose better; and you will listen better, and that's what an editor is before all else: a listener.

Observation

Though authors may express some initia as lessons, insights, and the like, I say all initia are, at their truest origin, observations. Grebanier claims that Ibsen, as he commenced *Hedda Gabler,* had in mind solely this abstract message: "A man or a woman lacking direction in life and with no work to do in the world may become a great menace to others." Only then did he conjure up the characters and situation that became the play.

I don't believe Grebanier. While it may be, just possibly, that Ibsen had not yet 'seen' Hedda or specific events (he regularly 'thought about' his plays for months before writing a word of text), it's clear to me that the generalization that comprised Ibsen's message had to be based on empirical evidence. Was Ibsen *born* believing this message? No. He observed. It was various ganged observations that he 'had in mind' when he then, rightly or wrongly, generalized.

One way or another, writers always start with an observation. Some of them, by the day they commence a given work, have phrased a general insight they are bent on promulgating. Others, however, report that they simply wanted to present the specific observed instance, a story: Let the reader generalize if he wants to. Still others say they started the book in order to discover, during the course of writing, what 'meaning' this transfixing observation held for them.

There had *better* be observation behind the impulse to write. There is a graveyard of mute, inglorious Miltons

whose only impetus toward paper was a love of words
and sentences. That love is a commendable thing, in the
best writers a necessary thing. But it is not sufficient.
Great readers have that love. Writing is a deceivingly
seductive art. More than any other, it leads the rapt spectator to believe he could do it too. Then, even worse, the
cunning infector so often deludes its host, leaving him
unable to see that he *hasn't* done it, that he is not the
possessor, but simply the possessed.

Tend You
that Obnubilant Moiety
of the Glabrous Will!

There are many essential aspects of fiction that I have failed to mention in this book—including style. Here is an oblique comment on style, occasioned by the earlier Note on arcane words.

Writing is, in a sense, a judicious compound of the familiar and the new. There must be enough of the familiar to make it comprehensible, but it's the new that makes it worth reading. Novelty alone is not sufficient, however; it must also *work*. It must have a reasonably sizable ideal intended audience that approves.

With every innovation—and innovation is certainly not confined to the level of diction and trope, though that's my focus here—the author is taking a chance. He *hopes* it will have an effect on his readers like the one it had on him when he thought of it (i.e., when imagination, serving prelibation, said, "How about *this?*" and sensibility approved), but he can't be sure.

To the degree that he is self-conscious the writer is jerked continually between glee and doubt. Can I really afford a five-dollar word like 'myrmecoid'? Or even a three-dollar one like 'sharded'? He fusses over the decision ("The goddam word is *right!*" "It's *not* right if it feels wrong to everyone else who reads it!").

Any writer realizes that if he can't make a decision, he'll never finish anything. His creative apparatus breaks

1 6 4

down. Imagination prattles on estranged and direction-less, sensibility starts vetoing everything, and prelibation just quits in catatonic doubt.

He needs a policy. Policy is to decision as prelibation is to imagination.

One policy is: Be bland; bland is safe, bland is easy. Bland is almost never new.

A better policy, the one I urge on writers who I know, or suspect, have a gifted imagination, is expressed in a telling line by John Barrymore: "You can only be as good as you dare to be bad."

Yes, it means you will continually be taking chances. There *will* be readers who want you to kill that ape with the oboe, get the diamonds out of the roast beef, cut 'myrmecoid' and 'sharded'. If the great majority of your bets fail with the great majority of those you hoped and believed you would succeed with, chances are your gifts are just not up to the job of being a publishable writer, someone with a justifyingly large ideal intended audience.

I talk of the 'ideal intended audience' as though it were a perfectly homogeneous thing, laughing and sobbing in unison, restively shifting simultaneously in its seats. But there aren't two people on this globe whose sensibility-prints are totally identical in every crease and whorl.

So the writer should live with the fact that though he may have a congregation that, on balance, likes his book, he won't please any two members in exactly the same way.

And if he would avoid chilling his creative apparatus,

he must also live with the fact he will please no single reader all the time. This includes his editor. But both editor and writer, if they belong with each other at all, usually accept this happily. In this book I have found myself incorporating ninety percent of the changes, or requests for clarification, expansion, etc., that my editors and commentators put to me. I understand why every single remark was made, but still I resisted on ten percent. I know George is right when he says my line about philosophers being daft (if they believe we think in words) is opening an unnecessary can of worms. But I keep it in—not because my sensibility says George is wrong, but out of my admitted orneriness, like my nip at William Gass in the next Note.

Sometimes a writer's stand *is* solely on sensibility. If I'm wrong about my audience's general—not universal—acceptance of the ape-with-the-oboe image, then I tell you I'm in damn bad trouble. Because I'm convinced it's okay. The best kind of editorial remark is the one that strums a chord already humming suspiciously in the writer's mind. There are other things in the script I *wasn't* totally convinced about, and if kibitzers on the manuscript had told me I had to get them out of there, I'd have probably said, yeah, yeah, I knew it, okay, out.

The writer has to be prepared to accept that someone out there will hate his whole book—diction, tropes, everything. He can believe that doesn't prove much. And each new thing he tries will find *someone* who rejects it.

But here's the peculiar thing. Most lay readers do not appreciate the variety of reader response. They tend to take *their* response as *the* response. The editor, if he's good and apt for the book in hand, does, enough of the time, react in a way that is *the* response. But still he's sensible enough to realize that even he, paragon that he is, may be idiosyncratic on a given point. The private reader, the non-editor, is usually absolutist.

"This is told in the present tense! I *hate* the present tense in novels. It's awful!" From "I" to "it's".

Thus the writer should not begin to wonder about his editor and wonder why he didn't notice such-and-such, just because someone corners him at a cocktail party and says, "I loved your book. Everything about it. Except that such-and-such. That was awful."

Doctorow says writing is like driving in the dark. I myself haven't felt I was driving. Walking, maybe. Sometimes striding, sometimes on nervous tippy-toe. But in the dark, yes. Often. Into the new.

Because Barrymore said to. Try it, he said, stroll into the night.

Noctambulic, wouldn't you say?

Shaggy Script Story

I stick by the implication in Part One that if there is no audience, past, present, or future, that would prize an alleged work of art, it is a failure. William Gass may assert that "the reader and his responses are not the test" because the books he call classics just "completely and absolutely *are*", but his argument is revealed as gibberish as soon as he begins talking about "beautifully imagined" characters and putting things in "where they will look well". Why care if it's beautiful or looks well if response to it is not the test? Once a year every publisher has some specter at the door, trilling to the receptionist that the shaggy script in his hands just "completely and absolutely *is!*"

To Circumlineate
Is Human

Words tend to hypostatize discretenesses to things, they circumlineate, and they have come to do so because, so goes one argument, the mind does too. But Bertrand Russell once wryly asked: "How long is an event?" Our inorganic brains—computers—are utterly confined to discretenesses. Some philosophers maintain that the ideas that our real brains entertain *are* discrete, with sharp borders to them; everything outside the border is not the idea, everything inside is. I don't think so, but I can't argue the case here. (Wittgenstein has already argued toward it in his analysis of the word 'game'.) This, though, we can accept: Words, uttered or written, are discrete. And we have to use these discrete things to sorcerize, call up, the indefinite spirits that are our thoughts.

That's what I'm doing in parsing the act of art the way I do. I don't mean to be making any statements about the actually particled reality of art; I'm only trying to enable us to talk about it. I do assert that the bull's-eye center of appetite is different from that of specific, determinate imagination. My language suggests discrete steps from one to the other—from salivancy to sense of effect-wanted to generic imagination to specific imagination—but I will concede that the noumenal fact of the matter may be a constant unbroken flow. This same assertion and concession applies to all the alleged distinctions I make.

A Prelibation

Let's say there comes a point in her novel where a writer senses that she wants the reader to feel the dominating power of the older man who has a young woman totally in his thrall. That's the text of the prelibation at this moment, and for good and basic reasons grounded in an understanding of how fiction works, she assumes she needs a scene. The characters have already been 'imagined' before this (and approved by her sensibility), so what she must conjure up now is an encounter, a kind of collision, in which the young woman comes out woefully on the bottom. But the writer also senses—prelibation *is* sensing—that it must not make the man seem brutal; by sheer weight and assumed authority and the right of ostensible wisdom, he steamrollers her. He is not totally opaque to what he is doing, nor is she, but *he* feels his point is right, so he will not temper his charge, and *she* feels she can have no legitimate objection in the face of what she accepts as his great wisdom and experience and underlying goodwill. Besides, she loves him and fears being unworthy.

All these things the writer senses she wants manifest in her scene; they must be impressed on the reader; she wants the reader to *feel* them, because one of her reasons for writing the book is to make readers feel and understand a fascinating domination relationship like this, and because it will prepare the reader to respond to later things in the book as they happen. Her current artist's presentiment is exactly as general as this: She wants the scene to have all these effects—and does not yet have a single specific act or utterance in mind for her characters. Does anybody write this way? Yes—very many. For them, conscious prelibation always precedes specific imaginings.

Prelibation by a Nose

As a rule, an implied prelibation *is* accompanied by a *general* imagining of what would satisfy, just as a salivancy in the reader frequently stimulates a more or less specific narrative hope. ("Oh, I hope Myra shows some sense for once!") And sometimes the reader's 'vision' pushes closer to specificity. ("I hope she gets out of the car right now!") How many times have we squirmed in our movie seats as the innocent girl obliviously sits and natters while the monster creeps up behind her?

Usually the writer is alert enough to know precisely what the reader is feeling—he has *intentionally* caused that feeling—and he may choose to provide what is longed for. In certain situations of peril, the genus of development wanted is as obvious and simple as: Escape! The writer takes his job to be that of figuring out specifically how. When there are complications, the writer, in imagining specific satisfiers, may add unimplied strokes the reader never thought of. (Myra not only gets out of the car; she grabs the ignition keys and throws them over the cliff so that Charles has no way of getting to town in time.)

And sometimes, the expert teaser, he will not provide immediate satisfaction, because he sees he can achieve an even better final effect by not doing so. This, too, may be thought of as unimplied prelibation; it is an intuition of a desirable effect to be had.

Indeterminate Prelibation

Perhaps we can get a glimmer of what an indeterminate prelibation is like by recalling how it feels when, say, just as we're leaving on a trip, we have the strong sensation that there's something we're forgetting. The mind's first effort is to fix the genus: Is it something I've forgotten to do? Or is it something I'm forgetting to pack?

Prelibation sometimes can be like a neon sign through fog: bright, beckoning, even familiar—but illegible. The artist tries to push on toward it. Sometimes it doesn't seem to be getting any clearer. Am I dreaming? he may ask.

The Problem of Hamlet's Sister

The most important single species of decision an author makes is the selection of his cast of characters. Reconsider any book or play, and try to picture it without certain characters, or with them changed, or with additional characters. The best books and plays give you the feeling that their cast was effectively inevitable. It had to be these and only these.

Well, how did the author know? Hamlet had no sister. Shakespeare knew. And he also knew that Ophelia had a Polonius. How? Books do falter because of irrelevant characters—and often you can indict the editor for that. Books also fail because of the lack of an essential character. And sometimes you can even indict an editor for that. But no grid, no textbook, will consistently tell how to decide whom to put in. Implied prelibation follows from what's already more or less imagined. Where does unimplied prelibation come from? From that unseeable, unplumbable deep the editor cannot even approach. And you cannot indict him for that. It is not even mappable by the rest of us, and yet our writers live there.

Pity the Great Writer

Authors, of course, suffer from their editors' failing at diagnosis. And, interestingly, it is the Great Writer, in particular the *master stylist,* who suffers most of all, because his editor is often so intimidated by the obvious artistry of the master that he will shrink from pressing a seemingly meretricious call to get the story right. Occasionally I encounter a published novel of noble richness of texture, but that is nevertheless palpably unsatisfying at book's end, and I'll feel a reader's exasperation as it occurs to me: If only he'd had a good and brave editor.

Book Review Editors and Book Reviewers

This is not what you expect.

Publishers regularly gripe about book review editors, either because a book isn't reviewed at all, or because, in the publisher's judgment, it was placed with a free-lance reviewer who was entirely wrong for it, and who therefore enjoyed it the way the Visigoths enjoyed Rome.

It happens the most with fiction. This is because the book review editor faces the same question the publisher should as he asks: Is this the right editor for this novel? If he has a nonfiction work in military history or crocheting, he can name his 'expert'. But almost everybody believes he can be an expert on fiction. In particular do novelists usually feel confident about volunteering their services as reviewers.

The book review editor's problem is the publisher's compounded. He has more books to assign, he seldom has the opportunity to get to know the free-lancers as well as the publisher does his editors, and in the end, if he has given the reviewer the job, he usually feels compelled to accept the reviewer's opinion.

Free-lancers tend to be literate and articulate, and one novelist can often reach poetic depths in shredding another.

But literateness and articulateness do not ensure that a reviewer is responding as the ideal intended audience for a book would. And in some sense, the review editor wants the appropriate reviewer just as a publisher does:

1 7 6

It's no good giving a mystery to someone who hates the genre. Yes, he's willing to run an unfavorable review, but he does it comfortably only if he can believe it's a reasonable and apt judgment that the book fails with its appropriate audience.

Too often, though, novelists who review are absolutists; if the book isn't for them, it isn't for anyone. Of course, novelists aren't the only ones so handicapped. The first review I recall of James Herriot's *All Creatures Great and Small* was by a librarian from Brooklyn who judged it not recommendable because who would be interested in barnyard humor like this?

I realize there are other legitimate views on this broad subject. In fact I was in favor of the famous John Ciardi demolition of Anne Morrow Lindbergh's poetry because I agreed with his reasons for thinking it needed doing. But when what's required is a review of the *book* rather than, in effect, a review of the prevailing *reception* of the book, I think most review editors would agree with the policy of finding a reviewer who is *apt*.

I flinch at betraying my calling by sympathizing with book review editors, but the trouble is I recognize their assignment and its unceasing difficulty, and I talk about it here because to understand *why* it is so difficult is to understand part of the publisher's task.

The *daily* reviewer, who often has to cope, all by himself, with a huge segment of the wildly variegated spectrum of what's being published, has to have the breadth of responsiveness of the entire staff of a medium-sized publishing house. The assignment is ridiculous, but the amazing thing is how close some of them come to pulling it off. A reviewer would be valuable for those readers who have learned through experience that *his* response is usually like *their* response, if all he did were to say, reliably, you'll like this one, you'll hate this one. Sometimes his value lies in simply naming the appropriate audience for a book: "If you like Le Carré [Ozick, Roth, Ephron], chances are you'll like this one." But usually he takes it as his assignment to say *why*. In other words, to diagnose. Tricky business, that, I've been saying. But I've also conceded that a clear articulation of response is tantamount to diagnosis and suggestion for revision.

When they do this well, and aptly nail a fundamental flaw in a book, they are puncturing not only the book and its author but, probably, its editor. But almost no editor will see it that way.

How to Break the News

Here's a basic rule for the editor every time he prepares an editorial letter or conference: *Always, when citing a fault, first express the effect, not the cause.* Don't say, "Rita is offstage for too long," or, "Mike does nothing to solve the crime," or, "There are too many locales," or "Perry is too much of a lightweight for Clara." Too often, the author's response will be, "But that was on purpose."

The editor's chances of prompting remedy are much greater if his citation starts with the symptom: "The reader has lost interest in Rita and also has the nagging suspicion the author has lost touch with his story and the reader appetite"; "The reader—because he feels disgust with Mike, who's supposed to be the hero but who comes out looking feckless and dumb—is frustrated and senses something basically misleading has been done to him"; "The reader feels confused, and his intensity of focus is shattered, because he can't hold eight different widely separated actions in his mind at once"; "Since Perry strikes the reader as weak, ineffectual, and dim, the reader is disappointed in Clara and dissatisfied with the whole resolution when she goes off with him at the end."

It's hard (not impossible!) for the author to respond, "I *meant* the reader to lose interest, trust, affection, focus, and respect!"

Consider an automotive engineer whose only report to the designer is, "You made the tail too blunt." The designer says, "I *wanted* a blunt tail." What the engineer had in mind and should have said is, "The car is supposed to be a racer but it is slow and inefficient. The cause is the blunt tail, which, at high speed, creates a trail-vacuum that is constantly sucking the car backward."

The underlying principle is: Absolutely nothing on the page can possibly be *intrinsically* wrong; the only criterion is the effect on the apt, intended reader. A misspelled, profane, and illiterate passage; a diffident, apologetic, minutely qualifying style; a brusque, didactic, autocratic pronunciamento—each of these, like ice cubes, bacteria, and saxophones, may be 'right' in some places and 'wrong' in others.

Matters Outstanding

What I've meant to do in this book is to suggest the potential range and intricacy of the craft. I haven't tried to explicate the whole business. I've only wanted to make the case: Look how much there is to *do.*

So there are matters besides style that I've hardly touched on. By *not* touching on a given subject, I don't mean to imply it's of lesser importance than the things I *have* discussed. Take style. There are moments for many of us as readers where style almost seems like everything we need. We know, like doctors watching a beauty contest, that beneath the lovely exterior there are structure and physiology that make it possible, but, during this sweet luxuriant flow, don't talk to us of calcium and enzymes.

I've mentioned elements that are necessary for drama, but I haven't talked about drama itself, what makes a scene in a novel powerful. For example, it is extremely hard to write satisfactory climactic fiction about a great musician, a violinist, say. And it's not because we can't quite hear him. It's because the essence of drama has much to do with a character's *choices,* and this requires our being able to see and appreciate the *alternatives* that he is addressing, and to understand the difference his decision makes. "That night, he played beautifully." Why? "Well, he just did." Yes, but even if we accept that it *was* different, we don't see what he did to *make* it different. This is why the courtroom lawyer is easier to write about than a swimming star. But this alleged insight should be squared with the fact that, *in film,* climactic drama with certain kinds of athletes *is* possible.

The editor's textbook that I lobby for would not be slim, as *this* book is.

Similarly, by concentrating solely on editing, and saying nothing about the other three assignments of the editor—acquiring, helping to 'publish', and supporting, comforting, and retaining authors—I don't mean to imply that those functions are of little importance. They are *immensely* important, but they are another subject. And those functions have been talked about in books already available about editing. Still, there is more that needs saying. "O!," sighs the editor at the altar of himself, "life is short, and editing is long."

GLOSSARY

One of the Notes remarks on the way that words tend to circumlineate the things they denote, when in fact the things are no more discrete and bordered than sub-atomic undulations are said to be. In this glossary, which is primarily intended as a set of jiffy reminders of the intent behind new or special usages in this book, I'll try to confess the sprawl of certain terms that, on their first appearance in the text, were put forth in ways that may suggest they are neatly squared-off notions.

Prelibation   The desire for a certain effect on the reader. It may or may not be followed instantly by an intuition of what item of narrative will cause that effect, and it's important to see that *that* intuition and the prelibation it is trying to serve are not the same thing. The intuiting of the narrative that will produce the effect-wanted is the work of *imagination*.

A reader can have a prelibation too, and often does. (See *salivant sensibility.*)

Prelibations do not necessarily arrive with perfect clarity. The writer frequently has to work at focusing the lens of prelibation in his mind.

The dimensions of prelibation vary from the level calling for individual diction and trope all the way up through characters, descriptions, scenes, and gads, to the level of effect-wanted by the book as a whole, which is the *master-prelibation.* The lower prelibations come in clusters and sequences that serve broader prelibations. Each prelibation more or less rigidly guides the prelibations below it, and the master-prelibation, at the top of the pyramid, is the overseeing guide of what to put into the book and what to keep out.

Axiom   The verbal expression of the master-prelibation. It follows that, insofar as any prelibation can be articulated, any prelibation may be said to have a potential axiom. If 'master-prelibation' were not already awkward enough a phrase for one day, we could sufferably talk of a 'master-axiom'.

Somacluster   The 'body-parts' of the novel—i.e., the characters plus the situation.

Situation   The character-circuitry plus the circumstance.

Character-circuitry   The lines of effect between the characters; the way they influence each other; the wiring that leads from the gads of one personality to the gad-receptors in another. To talk of the 'chemistry' between characters conveys some of the notion, but 'circuitry' has the advantage of more forcibly turning the editor's and writer's minds to greater specificity about the plug-to-socket fit. The aim is to identify and remedy such defects as colorful characters who don't 'connect' with other characters. A minor character with the sole function of occasioning characteristic action by a major character might be thus justified by his circuitry value.

Circumstance Setting plus circumstantial gads. Setting is era and locale. Circumstantial gads are those factors in circumstance that move the characters to action and are not simply inert background elements. (A dark and stormy moor may be 'inert' in that it does not cause the characters to act one way or another, but it can still have the value of helping to create a *mood,* as well as satisfying the reader's need to be oriented.) It's tempting to think of situational gads as dividing into personal gads (those of circuitry) and impersonal ones (those of circumstance—i.e., flood, famine, buried gold, job opportunity). The division may help clarify the notion of 'gads', as long as we don't get transfixed by questions such as: Is the unknown lunatic killer terrorizing the moors a personal or circumstantial gad?

Gad and gad-receptor A gad is a spur or stimulant prompting a character to act. A gad-receptor is an inclination or susceptibility to react to a specific kind of gad. Almost everyone reacts against the threat of drowning or starvation. But the promise of gold or power does not energize all people equally. Gad-receptors are as various as are the needs, hungers, fears, appetites, and susceptibilities of this world. A character need not be aware that he has a receptor for a certain kind of gad—thus *Rain* by Maugham. The personality of any strong character tends to have a number of elements that will act as gads. His strength may find a receptor in some character's readiness to be dominated; in another character, the reacting receptor may be pride. The gadded action in the first will be a going forward; in the second, withdrawal. Meanwhile, the strong man's disgust about the bigotry he sees is prompting him to actions that serve as a gad to the local redneck sheriff.

Personal 'motivations' such as greed, lust, ambition, and love of music are gads. So are physical fear, pride, shyness, love of quiet and tranquility. But each of these can serve as a gad-receptor. Sometimes the motivations are starters, sometimes they are reactors.

There can be personal gads that are not motivations in the person who has them: good looks, bad manners, high intelligence, black skin.

We are inclined to think of 'motivations' as entailing active awareness in the person who had them. If we accept that connotation, then there are gad-receptors that are not motivations—namely susceptibilities, the capacity to be moved by specific stimuli. Usually these susceptibilities, when exposed to the specific gad, become conscious and thereafter motivations: the innocent at the outset who learns that he is lustful, or homosexual, or addictive, or that he enjoys applause, music, or mountain-climbing. But there are even gad-receptors that never become motivations in this sense. Characters in novels have been drawn as repeatedly reacting with fits, fatigue, panic, or ecstasy to stimuli they can never control either by avoidance or pursuit.

Accident   Those events or developments in the novel that are not both willed and caused by a character. They are made to happen by the author. The author also creates the givens of character and situation.

Gustant sensibility   The responding faculty within the reader that tastes and judges.

Salivant sensibility   The responding faculty within the reader that feels appetite, curiosity, apprehension, craving for relief, for satisfaction, for completion. Thus, insofar as a salivancy may be thought of as the desire for a certain effect, it amounts to a prelibation. Often the reader will go beyond prelibation to imagination; he will envision the specific event he wants. The author may or may not give it to him.

When the craving—say, to know whodunit, or how the race comes out—has been palpably generated by what's already been supplied in the narrative, we say that both the reader and the author have an *implied prelibation.* But the realization of what effect would be great right here is not always so obvious. There are degrees of impliedness to these things, descending to levels of inspiration so subtle and obscure in their ingenious origins that we'd agree to say they're not implied at all. They are *unimplied.* These unimplied appetites of the artist (ranging from a craving that will be satisfied by a single word, all the way up to the shape of the whole book) are, with the imaginings that fulfill them, the sorts of things that have been called 'strokes of genius'.

I have not said much about imagination in this book because, among several reasons, there is little I can think of that the editor might do to improve it in the author. But in fact without the concrete imaginings to fulfill them, the best prelibations in the world are useless. (Except—another topic I left out—in collaborations. There have been joint creations in which one partner was the prelibator and the other the fulfiller.) And of course, for a great work, the *quality* of the imagination is equally important with prelibation and sensibility.

Initium   What the author had in mind when he began his novel. It can be the merest spark, with no cast, setting, or circumstance in sight. It can have varying degrees of substance above a spark, right up to a fully articulated axiom.

The point of all this anatomizing of elements in the novel—the parts of somacluster, gads, accident—is not to cater to a hobbyist's joy of classification. It's to raise the editor's and writer's awareness of the biological factors that are affecting the life of the novel.

It's meant to shed light on how each decision the writer makes may be having effects that he has not foreseen. Perhaps more to the point, it's meant to make him aware that decisions he is *not* making, things he's *not* doing, may be hampering the vitality and impact of his book.

At its dreariest, the study of these factors may be compared to the repeated exercises and experiments the student is put through in preparation for any art or science that will eventually require performance or activity from him, as distinguished from mere passive understanding. A chess player might compare it to the interest in setting up board problems. What if the pieces are arranged thus and so? But suppose this piece were a knight instead of a rook? Suppose I started with it two squares to the left?

I suggested that the best way to teach point of view was to ask the student to rewrite given scenes from a half-dozen different POVs. He doesn't come out of this labor realizing there is solely one POV that ought to be used at all times. Instead, he gets a feel for how various

POVs can affect the impression the reader gets. In other words, he comes to see how POV *works*.

The composer, the painter, the architect—even the chemist, the physicist, the mathematician—is drilled in the 'basics'. Some teachers are so limited that they mean their students to learn that this is how it should be done. The better teachers are acting on the premise that you can't, in a controlled, commanding way, depart from the orthodox before you grasp what the orthodox is. There is a theoretical argument that some otherwise innovative spirits are needlessly and forever ensnared by their training in harmony, anatomy and draftsmanship, Euclidian geometry. I'm not persuaded by the argument. I am persuaded by the evidence of how many valuable *innovators* we can think of who *were* exposed to orthodox training and displayed orthodox facility.

There is no doubt in my mind that the choice of the cast of characters is the most important decision the novelist makes, and that the choice cannot be optimally informed without attention to how they plug into one another, their circuitry. But the editor again and again sees characters chosen in effective isolation, or solely with consideration of the circumstance. Or solely with a narrow circuitry in mind and *no* consideration of circumstance. Gads end up with no receptors, and vice versa. Or couples gadded together dance to different beats on different nights in different casinos from one another.

And so on across the gamut of ailments a novel is potentially heir to.

The assembling and judgment of the somacluster is currently done with less clear-eyed craftiness than Henry James was bringing to bear a hundred years ago. I'm not saying that his particular architecture was best—perhaps Percy Lubbock proved, inadvertently, its limitations—but I am saying that the scope of the considerations is important. The writer and his editor ought to be conscious of how the factors I've mentioned all affect each other.

The last few lines of this glossary are directed solely to the writer. Pray you find a good editor, because, though you may be good, you are unlikely to be perfect. But before you even get to an editor, you should play with the factors above, check the fittings, try different parts, instruments, harmonies. You should practice, as the artist does who takes life-drawing classes and tries different mediums. Then you can experiment. When you have seen the need for, and the way to, serviceable master-prelibations for your novels; when you have mastered the orthodoxy of how different somaclusters can impart different potencies and directions to a narrative; when you are then able to use master-prelibation to help select your somacluster and guide your accident; you still will not have learned how to *do* it. But you will have learned how to allow it to get done.

Two closing observations. First, recall that these tools for analyzing the elements that determine the force and direction of narrative were devised for diagnosis. I strongly believe there are writers who will be able to use them during the creation of their novels, but those who can't may still find the tools can be helpful in understanding what they have done and are doing. Novelists diagnose too, not just editors.

Finally, a paraphrasing of the earlier allusion to being aware of the trade-offs you inevitably make as you

write. The writer who understands the basics of orthodox narrative has, by definition, a grasp of the benefits
allegedly achieved by each of its elements. It's certainly
true that some of the most triumphant moments in art
have come with departures from orthodoxy. But so have
some of its sorriest disasters. The author, through conscious choice or through ignorance, has sacrificed classic
satisfactions, and his bold replacements have failed. The
writer should have a firm understanding of what he is
giving up whenever he violates a basic precept or omits
an 'obligatory' element. He should be able to look at it
straight and clear as he makes his decision. He should be
able to say, "I understand what the orthodox move
would be right here, and what its effect would be. But the
effect of the move I want to make is preferable." He may
fail because his judgment is wrong, and that's certainly
lamentable. But there's some comfort in being able to say
you knowingly took your chances. To fail out of ignorance, because you didn't know what you were doing in
the first place, is pathetic and exasperating. And it's unnecessary.

Now that I look back on the last paragraph, I see it
all applies to the editor too.

PERORATION

Stanislavsky Edits

Picture an acting teacher or a director who, by putting canny queries (not instructions) to the actor about what the character would want, how he would react to so and so and such and such, what his fears are, who would cause him irritation, competitiveness, envy, pleasure, protectiveness, leads the actor to a fullness of insight the director need not have had himself and to a performance the director certainly could not have created.

Directors, coaches, and editors cannot (Fowles is right) teach you how to get there. But they can put you on the paths that *lead* there.

Sam Mussabini, Editor

In the movie *Chariots of Fire*, the trainer-coach Sam Mussabini sees Harold Abrahams run a hundred-meter dash and lose for the first time in his life—by one step. Mussabini approaches the despairing Abrahams, who has just declared aloud that he can't run any faster.

"I beg to differ, Mr. Abrahams," says Mussabini, smiling up at him and chewing on a cigar. "I can find you two steps in the hundred."

If you are a writer with the innate gifts, that's what a good editor might do for you. It should be what he is there for, it should be his life's work: *to find you two steps in the hundred.*

Jest Desserts

I suppose my experience is typical. People always told me publishers were thugs, and now I believe it. Two of my colleagues at St. Martin's whom I used to think good fellows, especially when they agreed to edit this book together, I now find miss no opportunity to criticize every line I write. They demand, with a mischievousness cunningly disguised as well-meaning concern, that I squander good energy in pursuit of their sinister fetish for clarity; they interfere with my concentration by pedantic badgering on the small-minded level of grammar, consistency, and logic; they spoil the pure Platonic beauty of abstraction by requiring what I can only think of as the vulgarity of concrete examples; they rob me of both my dignity and my hard-won distinctiveness of style by, in an oily, deferent manner that does not veil from me the smirking disdain behind it, insinuating that some of my freshest coinings are counterfeit, that my metaphors are emulsified, and that my noblest postures are less than the winsome tableaux I know them to be. They even (and I question their delicacy here) would have me believe that my exquisitely sculpted, league-long, pre-Raphaelite sonorities sound not like thunder but flatulence. In this manner have they laughed out some of my best stuff as they larked through a long bill of niggling, inconsiderate, and disheartening cavils that really make it a wonder a sensitive writer gets anything done at all.

And now, transparently feigning courtesy and regret, which I recognize as the joint glee and glower of jailers who have watched me at my last meal, these—and I'll not shrink from calling them the name they have only brought upon themselves and which they thoroughly deserve—these *editors* tell me my time is up. Deadline. Designers await. Typesetters. Printers. All woefully lining the corridors leading to that pitiless, naked scaffold where, before eyes leering, scornful, and indifferent, I shall be published.

Index of Names